CLIMBING
KILIMANJARO
WITH AFRICA'S TOP GUIDE

ERICK KIVELEGE

© 2021

Kilimanjaro Kutembea Publishing
Wind River Associates, Inc.
62504 Indian Summer Way E
Enumclaw, WA 98022 USA

&

P.O. Box 9518
Moshi Town, Tanzania

Or https://www.kutembeapublishing.com

Print Book ISBN: 978-1-09838-092-2
eBook ISBN: 978-1-09838-093-9

Printed in the Unites States of America

First Edition, June 15, 2021

To Our Ancestors,

May their peaceful spirits guide and comfort us on the trial until we see the light of the camp ahead, where we will find our meal, friends and our rest for the night, until the new day dawns bright upon the earth again.

CONTENTS

INTRODUCTION

Greetings from Kilimanjaro, the rooftop of Africa!

My homeland, Tanzania and East Africa, is the cradle of human civilization, a region of wonder and adventure like no other place in the world. Your journey here will take you to a faraway and magical land—back into time itself. The rhythms of this land and our culture will feel like drumbeats in your soul, awakening a connection that you share with long-distant ancestors.

This book about East Africa and climbing Mount Kilimanjaro is the first one written by a Certified Tanzanian Climbing Guide. There are many books about this magnificent peak, but none produced by someone who has climbed it more than 500 times, as I have. And there are no comprehensive books by a guide who was born and raised in East Africa, or who understands the culture and customs of Kilimanjaro and its surrounding villages like I do.

I will share the perspective of a Tanzanian, and as a highly experienced guide, I can teach you things you'll find nowhere else. As you prepare for your journey to my homeland—embarking on the adventure of a lifetime—this book will, I hope, become the most valuable resource you have.

I've guided thousands of clients up every route on Kilimanjaro, in all kinds of conditions. I've worked with people who came to me with a wide range of individual hopes and fears, strengths and weaknesses, and I've tried to understand them all. I can help you find your own path. Starting in the deep jungles near the equator, with monkeys gliding through the trees, you'll ascend to the snows of Kilimanjaro, the most remarkable journey in the world. You'll pass through every climate zone and have a chance to see dozens of different wildlife species, including many types of monkeys, birds, and some of the larger animals of East Africa.

Throughout these chapters, you'll find all the necessary travel, training, historical, cultural, and equipment information you'll need to successfully take on Kilimanjaro. You'll learn about the mountain and how to strive for its breathtaking summit at 19,341 feet, and you'll develop a deep appreciation for all that East Africa has to offer as a destination.

I'll also share the story of my own journey to a distant land—the United States—so you'll know that I understand your apprehensions about planning and completing such a long trip to an unknown place. I hope to help you have a better experience, giving you confidence that your adventure can become everything you've dreamed it will be.

CHAPTER ONE

WELCOME TO MY HOME!

The endless plains of Serengeti National Park.

Kilimanjaro is the highest mountain in the center of Sub-Saharan Africa, located in the country of Tanzania, very close to the equator. But it is much more than a mountain, or even a name. Virtually every person in the world knows the word Kilimanjaro.

It seems to most people like more of a feeling, or even an emotion of some sort. In every language and every culture, people pause when considering it. No one knows why this is so. The true meaning has been lost to the ages, something that adds to the mystery of this ancient place.

Roughly 4,600 years ago, the Pharaoh Khufu was building his Great Pyramid at Giza. Twenty-four hundred years before that, the waters of Lake Victoria flowed into what was Tanganyika, then into the River Nile and on to the ancient land of the earliest pharaohs in Egypt. But long before the pharaohs, there was human civilization right here, in the heart of Africa.

When you come to Tanzania, you should try to visit Olduvai Gorge in the Great Rift Valley, where scientists have found evidence of our first human ancestors, dating back 1.9 million years. Modern humans developed here 300,000 years ago; 40,000 years ago, my ancestors left East Africa and began to colonize the world, including Upper and Lower Egypt. By 10,000 years ago, they had traveled to and settled most of the continents of Africa, Europe, and Asia. You are a descendent of those original explorers.

By the standards of geologic time, human habitation of the earth is brief. Kilimanjaro was formed starting more than three million years ago, a long process that involved dramatic changes from continental rifting and volcanic eruptions. When the humans who originated here began their great migration to the far corners of the world, some ancient members of my tribe, the Chagga, settled on the slopes of Kilimanjaro, where we still live today.

Chagga (actually written *jagga*) roughly translates as "Places with very cold temperatures at high altitude." We are an ancient people, and this is an ancient land, which you will understand in a new way once you've experienced it. Your adventure and eventual summit attempt will be like a bridge from one life to another; you will never be the same again.

You probably bought this book because you've either made plans to climb Kilimanjaro or you hope to try it someday. Maybe it is just a dream for you, and that is fine as well. My first trip up the mountain, which now seems like a lifetime ago, happened in 1989, when I was 17 years old and found entry level work as a porter. Prior to that, my only work experience was on my family's farm in a village outside of Moshi, when I was still in secondary school. (In Tanzania, "secondary school" is comparable to middle school or junior high in the U.S.) I had an uncle who was a guide, and he thought I should try my luck working as a porter, carrying loads for others.

I'll never forget that first trip. It was extremely rainy and wet on the mountain, with water running down the trail. (Most guided climbs don't happen during the rainy season, so conditions are usually much better.) I had primitive gear, I was carrying a heavy load, my feet were soaked, and I was getting hypothermia from the rain and cold. I had trouble keeping up, and the other porters told me that if I fell too far behind and got lost, a leopard or a lion would probably eat me. Can you imagine being told on your first day at a job that a lion might eat you? That motivated me to move faster!

Things were tough for porters back then because of a lack of safety regulations, and we carried loads that weighed up to 40 kilograms (88 pounds). Today there are park rules that protect the porters. There are scales along the trail, so loads can be weighed each morning, and porters aren't allowed to carry more than 20 kilograms, which is about 44 pounds.

During that first day on the job, I swore that if I survived, I would never return to Kilimanjaro. But I kept marching forward, eventually caught up, and the weather improved. After the trip was over, I was proud of my accomplishment—plus, I got paid. I received $2 a day and $20 in tips. The total, $32, seemed like all the money in the world to me. It solved many of my family's immediate financial challenges.

Despite the vow I'd made, I knew I would go back. Someday I may return to farming, but today I am still a guide on Kilimanjaro. This has been my life's work, and in sharing what I've learned, my goal is to help make your trip a success in many different ways.

As for you, rest assured that you'll be safe from being eaten by a lion or a leopard, and that you can time your trip to avoid both of Kilimanjaro's two annual rainy seasons. We'll talk more about trip timing—based on weather and other factors—later in the book.

CHAPTER TWO

A BRIEF HISTORY OF KILIMANJARO AND EAST AFRICA

Mawenzi from the top of Kilimanjaro and the East African Plains.

Most books about East Africa start with the history of Kilimanjaro, usually delivered from a Western viewpoint. This is misleading, sometimes even disrespectful, so I'm going to start with a different approach, by telling you what it was like when I traveled to England and the U.S. in 2010. You'll see that my experiences, if presented as those of a "discoverer" rather than a visitor, can seem pretty comical.

I may have been the first person from where I live, a busy city of 200,000 people called Moshi, to visit Disneyland, and I'll admit I was amazed. When I was young, I lived in a traditional beehive hut that was made from mud and sticks and had a thatched roof, so going on the Pirates of the Caribbean ride was a pretty dramatic cultural change for me! In fact, when I went home, I was a bit of a celebrity. Groups of people would ask me to tell them about my trip. Some of the things I saw and experienced were hard to explain.

Likewise, you may have a hard time getting your friends and family to fully understand your experiences when you return from Tanzania. I had to do what you will probably do: I showed them photographs. When I told people about Disneyland, many friends and family did not believe me at first. But when I shared photos, they simply said, "We will be quiet now." They were genuinely amazed.

The history of Kilimanjaro is like this, in that very much depends on perspective. As I said, I was possibly the first person from Moshi to visit Disneyland, but I didn't discover it. It was there before I arrived. The same was true of Kilimanjaro—it was there long before explorers from Europe arrived. The Chagga were already here, too, and we had a thriving culture. European travelers were really just coming back to where their ancestors had come from.

With that in mind, here is a better way to think about the history of Kilimanjaro.

Most of the guides and porters are Chagga. Guides are required to speak English; this is a rule set by the government department that runs climbing here, at Mount Kilimanjaro National Park. When you hear us speak to each other, we generally speak Chagga or Swahili. Some guides speak French, German, and Spanish, but not many. Roughly half the people in Tanzania speak some English. About two-thirds speak a tribal language, but Swahili is our official national language, and it's one of the main things that unites us as a country.

Bantu was the original language of the people of Central Africa. People don't speak this language much anymore, but Swahili is a descendent of the Bantu and Arabic languages. It's a universal language spoken today by many people in countries throughout East Africa. Learning a few words and phrases in Swahili will make your trip more enjoyable.

When you meet someone on the trail, you will usually be greeted by "Jambo!"—which basically means hello. You'll start using it yourself, and you'll find that people warm to you quickly when you use this simple greeting. The answer is usually the same: "Jambo" in return. If you wish to ask how they are, simply say "Habari?" If they are well, they might answer "Nuzri," which means good, or they'll say "Hakuna matata" if they are doing really great. This means "no troubles." See? You are well on your way to meeting and talking to people on the trail.

But Swahili is much more than just a language. It also defines an ancient culture that dates back to the origins of human civilization as it existed around Kilimanjaro and the coast of East Africa. Long before invaders from other places began to come here, the Swahili culture of towns and villages had created well-established trading routes that went deep into Africa and out to the coast of what is now Zanzibar, a part of modern-day Tanzania. This is often referred to as the Golden Age of Swahili civilization. Early travelers described major Swahili cities as being some of the finest and most advanced in the world. Our culture pre-dates European and Western ones by a very long time.

The real truth is that Africans went on to discover and settle the rest of the world, not the other way around. Our ancestors were the founders of the great civilizations that came into existence along the way. When travelers from here got to Europe and settled that area, people later descended into religious superstition, fear, ignorance and violence for hundreds of years. This period is what is now called the Dark Ages in Europe. Knowledge, science, civility and history had been forgotten for a very long time when humans began to emerge from the Dark Ages. Over time, people slowly began to return to science, education and enlightenment.

They also started to go back to the places that they had come from, but they had forgotten their own history. They now saw Africa as a new land to be conquered, using their newfound weapons and lingering superstitious beliefs. These were actually the ancestorial lands from where all people had originally come, many tens of thousands of years before. The people who had remained in Africa had not developed the types of weapons that were invented during the Dark Ages in Europe, and then used during the 500 years of religious wars in Europe and the Middle East called the Crusades. This set the stage for the colonial period in East Africa and much of the rest of the world.

Western invaders initiated the slave trade in the 16th century, a very sad chapter in human history. They also tried to erase our culture and language. Families were torn apart and many never saw their relatives again. The Swahili-speaking people of different tribes resisted and fought the invaders for many years. These wars to regain our independence went on for a long time. In the end, we became a free and independent people once again in 1964.

The countries called Tanganyika and Zanzibar were reunited and became what we call Tanzania today.

Some of the older people here still harbor resentment from earlier times, and although most of the younger generation did not have any personal experience with that period, they are very aware of our history. During the period of German rule in this part of Africa—which lasted from the late 1800s until the end of World War I—there were efforts by missionaries to erase our culture and our language, and leaders of clans were executed. Many had their heads cut off. Terrible things happened to our people, most of which are far too brutal to mention here.

The British later controlled Tanzania—from the end of World War I into the early 1960s—and it was still difficult to endure being an occupied country. Guidebooks will tell you that we were a people discovered by westerners. This is untrue and deeply insulting. It is false history.

I share this with you because the era of colonialism is a very unpleasant subject for Tanzanians. We, our lands, and our mountains were not "discovered" by foreigners. Africans have always been here, and in fact my ancestors discovered the rest of the world during an era lasting tens of thousands of years. Please be respectful of this when you visit Tanzania. It is considered rude to do otherwise. Most younger people today are happy to live in a free country and do not dwell on the history of the colonial period, but I hope you know and understand that it was a very bad time for Tanzanians.

Many of the Chagga people here are Christian or Muslim. Missionaries came in 1848, but these faiths from other places are not the only beliefs practiced here. More than half of us still believe on Ghost, or what you may think of as God, a deity that predates Christianity and most other world religions by many tens of thousands of years. Today, the religious leaders of our pre-Christian and pre-Muslim customs are usually older people in Chagga society. They are very important to us.

When community disasters occur—for example, major fires that broke out on Kilimanjaro in 1997—tribal elders went to a place called Kifunika Hill, a small, inactive volcano on the slopes of Kilimanjaro that is sacred to the Chagga. The elders and most of us believe that Ghost lives on the summit of Kilimanjaro. They pray, offer animal sacrifices—of goats, sheep, and cows—and ask Ghost for rain. If you climb the Marangu Route up Kilimanjaro, you will pass Kifunika Hill along the way. Many visitors say they can sense that this to be a deeply spiritual place when they pass by.

Even though climbing and tourism are an important part of our local economy, Kilimanjaro is even more important as a part of our cultural and religious history. Please remember that the mountain is a holy place to us.

Religion is important to people in Tanzania, just as it is in other cultures and countries. But here, we also believe in the words of our national motto: Unity is the Power. Christians and Muslims here are like brothers and sisters, and in most communities we have churches and mosques both, standing side by side. Some families have both Muslim and Christian members, and no one thinks anything of it.

We are a nation of many tribes and religions, and we find that unity really is the power in Tanzania. This is why we adopted a common language for all tribes, and it's one of the many ways we have found our strength as a country. After Tanzanians regained their independence at the end of the colonial era, we renamed the top of Kilimanjaro. It had previously been called Kaiser Wilhelm Peak, but it is now Uhuru Peak. This is where we raised our new national flag upon regaining our independence. Uhuru means freedom in Swahili. When we look at the summit of Kilimanjaro today, we know that it is called Uhuru, and this reminds us of our freedom from the oppression of colonialism and those terrible times in the past.

It is high time that the "discovery" nonsense gets left out of guide and history books. So I will not recount those false tales; I will not mention the names of the colonial trespassers who ignored the true owners of the lands around Kilimanjaro and believed they had a right to trample the culture of the people from this ancient place. "Explorers" cared only about what they could steal from others and claim for themselves. I'm hopeful that, someday, these deeply offensive chapters and insulting stories will be deleted and replaced with the true history of our proud people and lands.

When you climb to the top of Kilimanjaro, you will share and feel that Unity and freedom for yourself. When you come here, you will be returning to the original home of all humanity. Welcome back!

CHAPTER THREE

THE LIFE OF A TANZANIAN CLIMBING GUIDE

Me and fellow guides.

I was born in Moshi Town District, Kilimanjaro Region, on June 14, 1972. Moshi is the starting point for most climbing trips to Kilimanjaro, because it sits right at the base of the mountain. There's a lot to see in Moshi; you'll enjoy getting to know it as part of your trip.

I have a brother who used to be a guide, but he went back to farming in 2014. We have no sisters. My mother didn't want me to guide because of the obvious dangers. "No, no," she said, "you will die from cold or rocks falls!"

I was sorry to upset her, but I really needed money to complete my education, and I kept pushing her to allow me to climb with my uncle, who was very experienced on the mountain. He died ten years ago, but he used to guide out of the Marangu and Kibo Hotels, popular climbing lodges in the village of Marangu, which is about 40 kilometers from Moshi. You'll find that many trips originate out of hotels like these; many of the best guides use them as a base of operations.

I needed money to pay for national exams that were required for me to enroll in high school. My mother was sick at the time, and my father had divorced her in 1974. So, during the Christmas holidays in 1989, I drove to my uncle's place and he got me my first job as a porter.

As I said earlier, the first trip was tough. We were using a popular route out of Marangu, and I suffered a severe headache while carrying a load between the Horombo Hut, at 12,200 feet, and the Kibo Hut, at 15,430. I had never walked on snow before, but I had to learn how to do it in a hurry near the Kibo Hut. On the plus side, I was surprised by the good food served to the climbers, which included rice, chicken, beef, and fish.

The money I earned solved most of my immediate problems, and I was able to go to Mazengo High School in Dodama, Tanzania's capitol, more than 500 kilometers southwest of my home in Moshi. During every major holiday—several times a year—I went back to Marangu to stay with my uncle and get more climbing trips under my belt. Friends who were already in the business helped break me in and offered encouragement. They explained that most trips are very dry, which was not always entirely true, but I appreciated their support.

After I completed high school, my family went through financial problems again, and I heard about a mountain guide training program at Kilimanjaro National Park, the huge expanse of mountains and forest that was formally established in 1973 and contains Mount Kilimanjaro. I applied and was accepted. I completed the training—which combined all the skill and fitness requirements needed to function professionally on the mountain—and in 1994 was granted a license.

My family was still unhappy about this idea, believing that the job was too dangerous. Kilimanjaro is a risky place—a number of people die on the mountain every year, usually climbers who suffer from high-altitude illnesses—but my family has gotten used to that part of the job over time. (My son, Collins, is thinking about becoming a guide someday.) One of the hardest parts of the job is being away from home. I met my wife, Beatrice, at the Keys Hotel in Moshi, where she was a hotelier. We were married in 2000 and our first daughter, Grace, was born in 2001. Our second daughter, Glory, was born in 2005, and the last was Collins, in 2007.

When you come to Tanzania, you will spend a lot of time with your guides and I hope you will get to know them well by the time you leave. Their life is not an easy one. This work, especially at very high altitudes, is difficult and physically demanding at times. The guides are responsible for your safety and will try to keep you comfortable in all types of environments and weather. They take this very seriously. Very few jobs require this much constant attention to detail, and it is stressful at times. We also have to do most of our climbing and guiding during windows of good weather, so we work very hard in these limited time periods. I hope you can understand how tough and demanding this job is, and that you will come to appreciate your guides and other climbing staff.

I live in Moshi now because of my job. I actually prefer to live in a smaller village nearer Machame, but Moshi makes more sense. I have to be there to meet other guides and clients, and to set up climbs.

Because I'm a guide, I make pretty good money by Tanzanian standards, but people also know that the work is seasonal and unpredictable, and they do not consider me to be rich. People who work in politics or government are generally better off in Tanzania, because those positions offer year-round employment.

That said, people in my family know that if they need something, I will share money when I have it. This is common in Tanzanian life. When I return from a trip, people will say, "OK, you went up the mountain last week, and you came back down, so you have something." That is how we do things here. We take care of others. This is Tanzania.

CHAPTER FOUR

LEAVING ON A JET PLANE—FOR AMERICA

Flying Virgin Atlantic from Nairobi to America via London.

Several years ago, I met a very kind couple from the U.S., Christopher and April Hurst. They hired me as their guide on the Marangu Route. They had traveled to Tanzania in 2005 and had climbed the Machame Route. On their return trip in 2009, they stayed at the old Keys Hotel in Moshi and signed on with me.

This book you are now reading originated from that climb. The Hursts had read many books about Tanzania in preparation for their trip, and as they described them to me, we were all disappointed by how inaccurate much of the information was. We wondered why no one from Tanzania had written an accurate book about climbing Kilimanjaro and traveling to East Africa.

After their trip was over, to my surprise and joy, Christopher and April invited me to come to America. I could not believe what I was hearing when they suggested it, nor could I really imagine that it might someday come true. Because of immigration restrictions, it's very difficult for anyone from Tanzania to go to the U.S. Visas are tough to get, in part because the government believes that most visitors from Tanzania will attempt to stay beyond their permitted travel period.

Christopher and April offered to sponsor me, promising government authorities that I would stay at their home and that they would make sure I complied with the terms of my visa. Christopher, a former law enforcement official and state legislator from Washington State, also got assistance from a Congressman he had worked with.

Even with this amount of help, arranging the trip was not easy. I had to travel all the way across Tanzania by bus, to Dar Es Salam and Dodoma, to be interviewed by U.S. State Department officials. They were kind, but also very thorough, and they had many questions. Finally, after a process that took several months, my visa was granted.

This trip seemed unreal to me. Jungles, lions, elephants, dirt roads, and mud huts were a normal part of my experience, and I wondered what life in a highly developed country would be like, and about things most Westerners take for granted. For example:

How can an airplane really fly in the air? For me, it would be like traveling to another planet on a spaceship. When you dream of coming to East Africa, you might also wonder about how different this land might be from what you are used to. A big part of any adventure is just the planning and anticipation of the journey.

My trip, and the entire process of getting to America, was an indescribable experience. It started at the bus station in Moshi. This was a very long and crowded bus ride, and I spent the whole time just thinking of what I might see and experience on my trip. I felt both excitement and apprehension as I looked out the window at the dusty road and saw my hometown fade into the distance. Being alone made it all the more difficult, but I knew that there was no going back now. I was on my way!

From Moshi, I went to Nairobi, Kenya, and spent the night in a hotel near the airport. My flight took me from Jomo Kenyatta International Airport to San Francisco, with a layover in London's Heathrow. Since this was my first time to fly, everything was new to me. I had to get checked in and go through customs and security. At passport control, a lady took my passport and told me to wait next to an elevator. Ten minutes later, she came back with it and directed me to the gate. I was nervous when she vanished with my passport, but it worked out OK.

To actually fly was nothing like I could have imagined, and it still seems unreal. Sitting for the first time in an airplane and feeling the power of the takeoff and flying through the air is something very special. At first, I have to tell you, I was afraid and unsure that such a huge plane could even fly. It seemed impossible, but after we took off, I could see that we were flying above the clouds. This reminded me of the view from high up on Kilimanjaro to the valleys below, but without the wind or fresh air on my face. I can never forget this. I still think of it often and smile.

On the first part of my trip, I got to know a friendly man sitting next to me on the plane. He was from India and he spoke Swahili! His family lives in Nairobi and he also had some family in the U.K. He offered me the aisle seat, since I have long legs. I'm very tall and the space between the seats is rather tight on the airplane. I have been used to a tough life, but I had not been prepared for sitting for 9 hours on an airplane. Sometimes I stood up to stretch my body, which helped a little. Other than that discomfort, I enjoyed myself in the air. I got delicious food for free and had friendly people all around me.

I arrived at Heathrow Airport, and I had never seen such a place, and I was amazed that people could have built something like this. I had plenty of time to look around, eat, shop, and even sleep: my connecting flight was 12 hours away. The price of food was very high, so I had to be careful with my money and decided that I wouldn't eat much again until the flight to San Francisco tomorrow. Then I settled down against a wall of the terminal to sleep for the night. I had already taken in a great deal of new experiences, and my trip had barely begun. I'll talk more about this story later in the book.

FINDING AND USING GUIDEBOOKS

Barranco Valley Camp on a beautiful day on Kilimanjaro!

On the surface, this task might seem simple—how hard is it to buy and read a book?—but it's not simple at all. There are many books about climbing Kilimanjaro, but too often guidebooks are written by people who traveled to Tanzania a time or two, did online research of some kind, and wrote an account filled with inaccuracies and culturally insensitive information.

Most people who come to Kilimanjaro have purchased and brought several different books. It's good to do plenty of research, but be careful: climbing conditions and guiding prices change all the time. A dated or inaccurate book could leave you with bad arrangements and unexpected expenses.

I will teach you how to plan your trip properly, and how to find a guiding service that will help you make your trip successful. You need to know what to look for and how to communicate with people here when planning your trip. One size does not fit all, and virtually every climber or group will have different needs. Some companies will try to make you fit into what *they* want. This is not a good idea. Good companies will find ways to accommodate you, and really honest ones might even steer you to another service if they think it will be a better match.

When planning a trip like this, the Internet is both a blessing and a curse. Yes, you can find just about anyone or anything there, but you know little to nothing about them, other than what they tell you. A lot of online "guide services" are nothing more than a scam put together by people who pirated photos and created a convincing website. I will help you avoid these pitfalls.

Many books and companies make a lot of money from the 50,000 people who come to climb Kilimanjaro every year. (This figure does not reflect what happened in 2020, when COVID-19 decimated international travel.) Guidebooks often give details on the companies, prices, and routes. But there is so much more that you need to learn before coming to Tanzania. Few of the books do a good job of helping you understand how to treat the people you meet, and following our local cultural norms. This is unfortunate, because if you understand and respect Tanzanian customs and people, they will welcome you like family. Previous guidebook writers have known and written very little about this.

Once you understand more about us, you will feel comfortable meeting and making friends. To give one example: Have you ever thought of stopping into a local bar in a place like Moshi and meeting people? Very few visitors ever do it, and guide services do not generally offer this as an experience. It's worth trying, though, and later in the book I will teach you what you need to know.

I will also be honest with you about your chances of making it to the summit. I recently saw a prominent website promising that any 60-year-old couch potato who smokes heavily can reach the top of Kilimanjaro with ease. They even have a picture of this imaginary client on the top. This is dangerous—an unfit climber like that could easily die. Climbing Kilimanjaro is a serious physical challenge. Run away from anyone who says otherwise.

Some companies offer trips up the mountain that take less time—three to five days, instead of the seven- to eight-day trip (or more) that I usually recommend. Unfortunately, gaining altitude too quickly can make your trip miserable, or even kill you. When people die on Kilimanjaro, it's usually because they ascended too quickly.

Guidebooks and websites will sometimes take money for recommending certain services without disclosing this arrangement to you. You may get information that is inaccurate and not in your best interest as a consumer. No guidebook or website can possibly suggest anything useful without knowing something about you first. I will explain a very different way to find services, guides, and hotels in this book, a system that will start with your needs and expectations.

Take the time to do it right. Proper training and preparation will serve you well. Having guided so many people to the summit, I know what you will need to succeed, not only on the mountain, but during the rest of your trip as well. In Swahili we say, "*Pole, pole*"—pronounced *po-lay*—which means "slowly, slowly." You will hear this from your guides all the time.

If you prepare in the right way, you will likely have a safe and enjoyable climb and a great adventure. To get there, you will need to read all of the chapters in this book, especially the ones towards the end. Take your time. Slowly, slowly!

I will not be providing you with endless pages and lists of companies who do trips to Kilimanjaro or East Africa. I am not selling space in this book to companies so they can be listed. I also won't provide you with pages of technical maps or GPS coordinates so you can find your own way. You will neither use nor need such information at any point on your trip. That is what your guides are for.

Pointless and usually inaccurate maps and GPS coordinates make our jobs as guides very difficult, because clients often want to argue with us about where we are and where we're going. Trust that we know what we are doing. Maps from guidebooks (which are usually wrong) and GPS coordinates also encourage bad and illegal behavior by clients who decide to wander off on their own, or who decided they can illegally climb Kilimanjaro without Tanzanian guides. This is very dangerous.

In this book, I'm including a few maps so you can see the general layout of Kilimanjaro and the routes, along with some of the major camps and features. They are not intended to be technical— instead they're meant to spur your imagination and boost your general understanding of the different routes. If you ever need a map or GPS coordinate while on your climb, you have booked the wrong guide service and have gotten advice from the wrong guidebook. A good book will help you arrange the right trip, so you don't have to worry about getting lost in the first place, which in truth is difficult to do on Kilimanjaro anyway.

Don't get me wrong. It's OK to look through a number of sources before coming to Tanzania and Kilimanjaro, but be aware that virtually all the books on the market contain significant errors and omit much information you need for a successful trip. Only someone from Tanzania can provide you with accurate information about our lands, culture, and people. If I wrote a guidebook for visitors to your hometown, how accurate would it be? Keep that in mind when doing your research.

If you are planning your trip well in advance, I will try, if I can, to answer your questions via email, depending on how many people write me after this book is published. And who knows, if I have an opening, I may even guide you to the top of Kilimanjaro myself, since that is still my primary job. As you get underway, I'll say this: *Salamu rafiki! Nakaribisha kwa kilimanjaro na kupanda kwa mafanikio!*

This means, "Greetings, friend! I welcome you to Kilimanjaro and to your climb to success!"

SEARCHING FOR GUIDES AND BOOKING YOUR TRIP

Guides meeting with and briefing their clients at the old Keys Hotel in Moshi.

Tanzania takes tourism very seriously. This industry brings a lot of money into our local economy, and making sure tourists have a safe and enjoyable trip is important to people here. Our Tanzanian National Parks officials constantly strive to meet this goal.

Guides have to be licensed by the National Park Service and are carefully trained. They receive instruction in fitness, medical issues associated with climbing, the flora and fauna found on different regions of the mountain, safely getting around on glaciers, and many other areas of skill and knowledge. Selecting a good, qualified guide is very important to the success of your trip.

When you climb Kilimanjaro, you will not only have a licensed guide, but porters and a cook as well. A good cook is crucial: they're trained to make food that is not only good to eat, and nutritious, but safe. Travelers don't have the same built-in immunities as Tanzanians do, so the handling and serving of food must be done with great care. The last thing your guide wants is for you to get sick on the mountain.

When you start checking out operators and guiding companies, be careful not to believe everything you read. There are operators who will try to cut corners, and if you see a climbing package that's extraordinarily cheap, that's almost always a bad sign. It's possible to climb Kilimanjaro illegally—without guides or permits—but please do not even think about doing it. You will not be successful, you will not have a good time, you could get sick, and you may die. Don't become a statistic by breaking the rules or using discount operators.

The rules and systems put in place by the Tanzanian government and Tanzanian National Parks are there for your safety. Please be careful and use their knowledge. You can always reach out to the National Park Service and check to see if you are booking with a good and properly certified company. Do not pay any money until you're sure that you're working with a trustworthy outfit.

In my experience, you'll get the best results if you do your research and hire guides *before* you get to Tanzania, whether you book locals or hire a foreign guide service that offers trips here. Some travelers come to Tanzania and simply hire a guiding company at the airport, or they wander around Moshi in search of a local guide. You can do it this way, but it's more of a gamble.

Don't forget that, by law, you must always end up working with a Tanzanian guide, no matter who you your book with. It's very important to the government of Tanzania that guides and their companies be reputable. If a person has cheated you, let someone know at Tanzanian National Parks. They will actually assist you in taking that person to court. But of course, the best thing is to avoid using disreputable guides in the first place.

If you wish to hire a Western guide company, you can usually count on a trip that features skilled guiding services, reputable accommodations when you're not on the mountain, and good cooking. Another benefit: communications will be easier when you're setting up the trip. However, Western companies generally charge more for these extras. As you now know, you will have Tanzanian guides on your trip, but Western guiding services will also send their own guide or guides on the trip as well. You will have probably met them prior to coming to Tanzania, and they may even travel with you at some point along the way to Africa. The guides who do international climbs usually have significant experience. They will work closely with your Tanzanian guides.

Western guiding companies tend to be fully up to speed on first aid and medications, and they know how to handle injured or ill climbers. Most Tanzanian guides have gone through some level of medical training, but not all of them have been trained to the same standard. This is a topic you should research carefully when you're choosing a company.

There are roughly 200 separate companies that offer trips on Kilimanjaro. That is a lot, and there seem to be more all the time! If you include companies that do safaris and other types of trekking, there are probably 500 altogether.

The number of choices can seem overwhelming, so it helps to factor in your particular needs. Whether you're traveling alone or with a group of people you know, there's a possibility that a tour operator will merge you with other people who you don't already know. You will be on the mountain a pretty long time, and you may or may not care for the company of some of your fellow travelers. Think about this ahead of time when planning your trip. Not everyone will be fit enough to make it to the top, and different companies have different standards about who they allow on their climbs. You need to know about these. Some companies have strict standards of preparation and conditioning to make sure they maintain a high success rate, both for the safety of their climbers and for their advertising and reputation.

A single person can call an operator and book their own guide, cook, and porters and not go with another group at all. But remember, this approach will cost more—roughly doubling the price you'd pay if you were part of a larger group. Some people don't mind paying the price, because this can be a better way to experience the mountain.

Let's break down some typical costs. (Note that these are prices as of June of 2021, so remember that they will change after that date.) If you book through a Western guide, you might pay somewhere in the range of $5,000. If that company hires my services, they'll pay us around $3,000 to $4,000 for the whole trip, and we will provide everything that's needed. So a $5,000 climb is really costing about $3,000 to $4,000, but you will get plenty of value for that higher price, in the form of competent guides, capable porters, good cooks, and better advice on preparation.

Because of their high success rate on the mountain, companies that provide services like this may be booked a year or two in advance, perhaps longer.

Booking directly in Tanzania can also be a great option, and it's the way most people do it. For this service, don't plan on bargaining. When you call guide services in Tanzania, they'll give you a fixed price based on the type of experience you want. If you ask for a lower price or negotiate on a price, it's highly likely that you'll end up decreasing the safety and quality of your climb, because you'll get less experienced guides, cooks, and porters. The best guides won't lower their prices at all. Decreasing the price not only results in less experienced and knowledgeable guides and staff, but often results in decreased language skills for your staff as well. This can complicate your trip, especially if you encounter difficulties on your climb.

I do not recommend using the lowest-cost climbing services. There are some companies that might ask you to carry heavier loads, or do some or all of your own cooking. I think that's a bad idea, because you need to stay focused on the challenge of climbing the mountain.

If you can bring multiple people on your climb, you can reduce the price for each person. The reduction can be significant: as much as a $400 per person, sometimes more. So you might go from roughly $3,200 to $2,800, without cutting safety or quality. In any event, you should shop around with different companies and compare prices.

If I am available, I can take you, but I am pretty busy during peak climbing season, and I no longer guide during the rainy seasons. (I'll say more later about the best times to climb.) And please be aware that I only earn money from climbs I guide. Many people, and some guidebooks, earn extra fees by recommending particular services, hotels, or guides because they are being paid to do so. If I give you any advice, you can trust that it's something I personally believe in. I also happen to know a vast majority of the guides on Kilimanjaro and am very familiar with the best ones.

Now let's talk more about the specifics of booking your trip. A good place to start is right at home: find out if somebody in your town or city has climbed Kilimanjaro and ask them about their experiences. Check with local outdoor companies like Recreational Equipment Inc. (REI) to see if they can connect you with climbers from your community who have been here. People are usually all too happy to share their stories and, even better, their photos! These will also prepare you for your trip by seeing what to expect.

Nothing really compares with this type of analysis, especially if you have similar expectations for your trip as these people did. People who've done it already are good judges of climbing operators and hotels. If their trip wasn't what they hoped for, they can tell you why. You may talk to people who went through disappointments, but it's likely they'll have met other people who didn't. This is more common than you might think. Prospective clients who came from referrals have often contacted me over the years.

U.S.-based companies like Rainier Mountaineering Inc. (RMI) and International Mountain Guides (IMG) have been doing these trips for a very long time. There are others, and I am just using these two as examples, not because they are the only game in town. They have not paid me to talk about them.

But I also know that these are good operations. I have known and climbed with some of the leaders from these two companies over the years, including people like Phil Ershler, George Dunn, and Eric Simonson, who have climbed all over the world, including on Mount Everest. Using this type of company carries the benefit of working with established, experienced people whose reputations can be checked. You will generally feel safe about the services they provide, at every stage from preparation to summit day.

Another positive thing about these outfits is their commitment to acclimatization. For example, RMI and IMG only do seven-day climbs, and they will not even book a shorter one. Doing it this way is safer than trying to get up and down in a hurry to save money.

But as I mentioned earlier, RMI, IMG, or any other company from outside Tanzania, will not be the only ones guiding you on one of their trips. Only local guides are authorized to do this, and you will have Tanzanian guides, cooks, and porters on each and every trip. Generally, these companies, if they've been around for a long time, know the best people to work with in Tanzania. They also book good hotels and transportation.

Now back to the downside: cost. You will definitely pay a premium for this type of service. In 2020, the price was roughly $6,800 for a climb and safari, and around $4,800 to $5,000 for just the climb. I would strongly suggest doing the safari when you come here. You've traveled a long way—why miss out on the most astonishing wildlife areas in the world?

If you book directly with Tanzanian companies, prices for the climb alone will range between $1,000 and $4,000, depending on the type of services you want. I would stay clear of anyone telling you they can book your climb for around $1,000. It can't be done well or safely anywhere near that price. I'd recommend looking at $2,500 to $4,000 as a target price for a fairly well organized and safe trip with a good company. If you want extras or other types of services, you can go up from there. This price range will also include the park fee, but of course not a safari.

Also be wary of websites that offer to find guide services for you and "impartially" recommend such services. You don't know them, and they know nothing about you. When you use such a service, you only know what they say on their website and nothing more. They may not even know anything about Tanzania or Kilimanjaro. But they will be happy to take your money, credit card, or personal information. Do your own research and do not fall for scams. It's easy to make a website look good, but all too often there's nothing good behind it.

Many people behind these sites haven't actually done the climbs themselves, and they simply re-book you with other existing operators after taking their cut from your money. The problem here is that you are not even dealing with the guides or guiding service yourself, but only with a website or phone operator. Who knows where they are even from? This is where the internet is the most dangerous and misleading. They can also take a premium price and book poorly qualified and poorly paid staff. You will never know it until you are in Tanzania, and then it is too late.

If you decide to book a trip with a Tanzanian company and want to safely save money, you'll find that many good climbs and safari packages are hotel-based. There are many really nice hotels in the Moshi area and some in Arusha, a large city about 80 kilometers west of Moshi, closer to the base of Mount Meru. The packages they offer, on the surface, tend to be a little more expensive than independent operators, but they are all-inclusive. This means even your meals and hotel stay, as well as transportation, are included in the price.

Calling a reputable hotel can be a safe way to book your climb. They will always have someone who can speak your language. Good hotel operators carefully explain their compliance with Tanzanian laws and National Park rules regarding the treatment of porters and staff. This is very important. Your guides, cooks, and porters will work very hard for you, so you need to make sure they are treated fairly and paid properly if you book them through a hotel.

You need to make sure that your additional days in Tanzania, prior to climbing, are also booked up front. Later, I will tell you more about the hotels, since I have been to all of them over the years.

I will let you know about one last scam on the internet these days. Any company that counts any or all of your days in Tanzania that are not on the mountain, as part of your "climb", is not being honest with you. Only days spent actually climbing on Kilimanjaro will count toward proper acclimatization. I have seen many companies who advertise climbs of a specific length, only to find that the first day or two are actually days that you traveled to Tanzania and were not actually past a Tanzanian National Park Service gate and climbing. This is very dishonest. Your briefing day and hotel stay in Moshi or Arusha are not climbing days. An eight-day climb means seven nights in huts or tents on Kilimanjaro, not sitting at the bar having a beer in Moshi. Be very careful about this. You will not be acclimatizing while having a been in town.

In summary, let's go over the main points one more time:

*Cost is often the best indicator when you're searching for reliable climbs as part of a package. Be sure to think about combining your safari to our outstanding Tanzanian National Parks. You will be glad you did!

*Do not book short climbs or do business with companies who offer them. They are unethical and unsafe. Never do a short climb. Five days or less should be avoided altogether, six days is the bare minimum, and seven or eight days, or even more, is best. If you need to rush your trip, you should not come. It's better to wait until you can do it right.

*Do your research! Talk to people who have climbed with the company you're thinking of hiring. Such people should not be hard to find, no matter where you live.

*Do not place too much trust in the Internet. It is full of crooks and scams that can waste your money and put your life at risk. Much of what you'll find is untrue and written by people who have no personal knowledge of guiding on Kilimanjaro. Some guidebooks are not much better.

*If you can afford it, think of booking through a mountaineering company in your home country, one that is established and reliable. It will cost a bit more, but everything you need will be provided, including information about training and preparation. Ethical companies will not even allow you to book with them if they do not think you will have a safe and enjoyable trip.

*You can save money by booking your trip yourself with providers in Tanzania. Get to know them well ahead of time, and make sure all your questions are answered before making a payment.

*When using references from others who have been here, make sure you have the same expectations as they did prior to their trip. Actual references from your home community are the best way to judge a specific guide service or hotel.

*You can also check with Tanzanian National Parks if you have questions about an operator. They can tell you if you are dealing with an operator who they know is illegal, unsafe, or not authorized to guide in the Kilimanjaro National Park. Remember: they want you to have a safe and successful climb as well.

CHAPTER SEVEN

PHYSICAL AND MENTAL PREPARATION

Welcome sign at the Marangu Route Gate.

People come to Kilimanjaro for many reasons. Most find it deeply satisfying to stand on the highest summit in Africa and think about the work it took to get there. It's no easy task, and fewer than half the people who start will make it to Uhuru Peak. If you follow the guidance I provide in this book, your chances of success will be significantly higher.

There are many reasons for this low rate. The most common is a lack of preparation, combined with unrealistic expectations. If you have trained properly, your chances are very good of getting to the summit and having a safe and enjoyable climb. But people arrive in various states of readiness, sometimes with strange ideas.

For example, it's become increasingly popular to get married on top of Kilimanjaro. I've had clients who wanted to do this, though I advise against it. For one thing, you have to make sure that everyone you want at your wedding, including the person you intend to marry, can make it to the top. Remember that the average success rate is 50/50. If one of you fails, your wedding might not work out so well! Kilimanjaro is not a good place to get married.

The air is thin at 19,341 feet, and summiting Kilimanjaro can affect your cognitive functions. I once got into a long argument with a client who was convinced that a cluster of rocks ahead of us on the trail were tents, and that I was leading him in the wrong direction. What happened to him is not uncommon. Occasionally, people can become delusional while they're at altitude, but this quickly passes as one descends.

One man from Australia had a death wish and told me he planned to kill himself by jumping off the backside of Kilimanjaro after reaching the summit. Fortunately, I was able to keep him from carrying this out. That might have been his plan all along—who knows?—but my point is that altitude can do unusual things to people.

Meanwhile, some climbers just act silly. I once had a Russian client who, near the summit, decided to find a large boulder, so he could hide behind it and go to the bathroom in private. After a few minutes, he suddenly came out from behind the rock, totally naked and drinking from a bottle of vodka. He proceeded to the summit, where he wanted his picture taken.

I would not recommend doing this, either. The cold can be dangerous, and it will not help enhance the photo of a naked man, if you know what I mean! Vodka is never a good idea at altitude, nor is any alcoholic drink.

People want to do silly things all the time. Running to the top and back down is one—not a good idea, no matter what shape you are in. Bicycling up or down the mountain is also popular, as is doing some "extreme" thing like wearing a chicken suit during the climb. I suspect that the Internet has spurred some of these foolish ideas, and I would advise that if you want to do something like this, please don't come. It will not make you famous. It is disrespectful.

Climbing Kilimanjaro is a serious endeavor, and you should respect others when you're here. Many of those climbing the mountain are seeking a deeply personal experience and appreciate fellow climbers who behave respectfully. Rescue is very difficult on Kilimanjaro, and reckless behavior can imperil the lives of other climbers, rescuers, guides, and Park Rangers. People die on the mountain every year, and many accidents happen because of irresponsible, unnecessary activities. Kilimanjaro is a holy place to many Tanzanians. Respecting it will bring you good fortune.

To do Kilimanjaro right, think about your goals and carefully plan your trip. Talk to others who have done it. Devise a reasonable and responsible budget. Above all, do your physical training, which should be part of your plan from the beginning. If you can't afford to make the trip safely just yet—either for monetary or fitness reasons—save your money and train more before you go.

As I've said, fast trips are unsafe and are rarely successful, and you should plan to work in one or two extra acclimatization days during your climb. This involves staying at the same camp for two or three nights, going on a hike each day, and heading back to your camp in the evening. Doing this is worth the extra time: it's the best way to make sure you are acclimatizing properly. You will feel much better and have a greater chance of summiting.

Some longer climbs automatically build this process into their itineraries simply because of their distance. Many climbers are choosing to book longer climbs these days because of their high success rates, but of course almost all the routes are fairly equal and can have a high success rate, if climbed properly.

Another good idea: spend a day or two in town before starting your climb, so you can recover from jet lag and adjust to your new surroundings. If you get off a plane and start climbing the next day, your first couple of days on the mountain will be much more difficult. If you're well-rested, you'll be able to enjoy the sights in the jungle portion of the climb, at lower altitudes. This part of the trip is really fun, but not if you're feeling queasy and tired. Our latitude—very near the equator—takes a couple of days to adjust to, as does the time change. Later, I will share specific ideas about what to do during this period.

Before traveling to Tanzania, you should see a doctor, who will assess your health and determine whether you have any condition that might make climbing too dangerous. Some maladies that are not risky in daily life can become much more serious at altitude, and there are no medical facilities on Kilimanjaro. It's a long walk out. Even if you get off the mountain, medical facilities in Tanzania are not like those in the country where you've come from. A serious illness will necessitate air travel to your home country or somewhere in Europe. A previously undiagnosed heart condition or other serious illness is not something you want to find out about on Kilimanjaro.

If you need special equipment for your climb—like for sleep apnea or some other condition—you'll need to look at your options and decide if the risk is worth taking. Personally, I don't think anyone should risk his or her life to do this climb. And if you get sick or suffer an injury, you will also imperil your rescuers and other climbers who might try to help you. Phil Ershler of International Mountain Guides is famous for saying that he would not choose to get frostbite, even on the very tip of his little finger, as the price for summiting any peak. Phil and I think alike on this. Your trip should be fun, and you should not take any unnecessary risks.

Most people climbing will experience some level of altitude sickness while climbing; even experienced climbers and guides can feel it. The best cure is descending to a lower altitude and taking time to adjust. Medications like Diamox can also help, but don't use them without consulting your doctor first. More on that later.

Once you're cleared to go by a doctor, improving and maintaining your fitness is crucial. If you don't exercise regularly, you can still have a safe and successful climb if you work in advance to get in shape. This may take several months, so you should plan it out and get started early.

There are different types of fitness, each important. The first, of course, is physical fitness, and I think you'll find that hiking up and down hills is the best type of exercise, because it's so similar to what you'll be doing on Kilimanjaro. Each day up there, you'll hike on all types of terrain, at different elevations and in different climate zones, from deep jungles to barren areas with huge boulders and snow. In all cases, you'll be hiking for many hours each day.

Keep in mind that your guide will want you to hike very slowly: *pole, pole,* remember? Your guide will remind you to move slowly by saying these words often. It may seem odd to walk at this pace, but that's how you stay healthy and acclimatize properly. When you start your climb, it will seem unusual to walk at this pace. You can prepare by practicing at home in your training. This just means walking slowly on steep terrain at times as you go up.

At home, a good measure of fitness is whether you can do a typical strenuous day hike. If you're able to walk up reasonably steep terrain with altitude gains of 1,000 meters (3,000 feet) while wearing a 25-pound pack—and you can do this on successive days—you should be more than ready for Kilimanjaro. You may not quite make it to this level of fitness, but set it as your goal.

On Kilimanjaro, you won't have to carry your own supplies, just your daypack items like water, rain layers, and snacks. Porters will carry the rest of your gear. Still, it's good to train with weight on your back, to help build endurance. Try to increase the weight you carry as you get stronger. When you get to Kilimanjaro, you will be carrying much less, and it will feel great!

Your first days on Kilimanjaro will probably seem much easier than your training days back home, because, again, you will be going slowly and with much less weight. What you are working toward is your summit day, the physical climax of your trip. The more prepared you are in advance, the more enjoyable the entire trip will be. Although challenging, climbing Kilimanjaro is not the Olympics, and you will not be in a hurry.

You do not need to carry weight downhill on Kilimanjaro, so don't bother wearing out your knees and joints by doing this back home during training. Carry water bottles on the climb up, and then empty them at the top, so you come down lighter, protecting your joints. Train smart and efficiently. Never court an injury when preparing for this trip, especially within a month of your departure, at which point you will not have time to recover properly. I have had clients who showed up with injuries they suffered by pushing too hard just before traveling here. You do not need to do this.

Try to train in a way that's similar to how the climb itself will be. You may take a break for two or three days, but after this pause, try to train daily for a week. Before coming to Tanzania, do several seven-day stretches of training to see how you feel at day's end.

There is a mental discipline to this as well, and I believe that 80 percent of summit day is really in the mind. Some climbers like to say, "Set a stout heart to a steep hillside," and this is certainly true on summit day. Part of that mental discipline involves already knowing how it feels to exert yourself at a maximum level for five or six days in a row.

The lower part of the mountain is 90 percent physical and 10 percent mental. Summit day will be about 80 percent mental and 20 percent physical. This will probably surprise you. By the time of summit day, you have already made it to the high camp, so you are well on your way to the top, but this is where you must have mental reserves and a good plan for what is always a difficult stretch. I have seen many people who had used up all of their mental reserves and didn't have enough left to make it to the summit. Some were in great physical shape, but they didn't have the mental game to keep going.

Why? One reason is simple: the strain of living on Kilimanjaro for a week. Many people have never slept in a tent or in small huts for a long period of time, and not being familiar with this routine can wear them down. Others have trouble sleeping enough and get worn out.

It might seem odd to you now, but if you have a back yard, I recommend sleeping in it for a week. It takes an adjustment; even recreational campers usually don't spend this many days in a row in a tent and sleeping bag. Do it ahead of time and it will feel more familiar on Kilimanjaro. You might also want to see what it feels like to not shower for a week. Your family will probably not let you back inside your home to sleep in your own bed until you finally wash! But this is what you will feel like on summit morning at high camp.

If you don't have easy access to hills or mountains, stair-climbing in tall buildings is a good alternative, mixed in with other types of exercise like running or biking. I have seen people who had developed great endurance and strength from running and biking, but they had not developed the muscle groups needed for the terrain of Kilimanjaro. They had a much tougher time. I have known climbers from flat parts of the world who did stair climbs as part of their training and did great. Working out in a gym can be helpful, and I've also had clients who used Stairmasters to effectively build endurance and the proper muscle groups necessary for this trip.

Another type of fitness involves acclimatization. If you live in an area with big mountains, like the Cascades in Washington, the Rockies in Colorado, or the Alps in Europe, you should spend time hiking at higher altitudes, to get a better workout and a sense of how your body performs up there. It's OK if you experience some altitude sickness—most people do at some point—because it's better to have experienced this before coming to Kilimanjaro. You will also learn that early symptoms can be dealt with, fairly easily, in a number of ways. You will not actually keep this acclimatization for more than a couple of days, so it does not accumulate. But the experience of building up fitness at altitude creates confidence and mental toughness.

Often people will get headaches, nausea, or even a feeling like the flu at altitude, and these are signs that it's time to take a break. Experienced climbers who come to Kilimanjaro do not let it bother them too much, unless a more serious condition like pulmonary or cerebral edema is setting in. They have felt common

An outhouse on the Marangu Route. Be prepared!

high-altitude sickness before, and they know how to deal with it. Simply drinking more water or eating something may be enough to help. Some climbers like to have a pocketful of hard candies to suck on during a hike. This helps them keep their energy up. Whatever happens, it's important to let your guide know how you're feeling. Good guides will ask often.

It's also important to go slow and stay hydrated and to eat food as you climb. Descending to a lower altitude can cure high altitude sickness very quickly. Once you acclimatize for a bit, you can ascend again. Just taking a short break, drinking water, and eating will often do the trick.

You won't be using oxygen on Kilimanjaro. It's not a safe practice, since there won't be a reliable supply for you if you get into real trouble. If you find you need oxygen, then you've already gone

Inside an outhouse, complete with a broom,
in case you or someone else makes a mistake.

too far and have not acclimatized properly. If you can't climb without oxygen, you do not belong on this journey, and you shouldn't climb with a company that offers oxygen to help you get to the summit. More on that later in the book.

Once you get underway, the early parts of your climb will be in a jungle, with deep foliage and monkeys in the trees watching as you pass by. This is a beautiful part of the trip and most trekkers find it very interesting. Some people are frightened by the jungle, but it is safe, and the animals will not eat you. It can sometimes rain heavily for a short time in this environment, so be ready to hike in a heavy downpour. Chances are that you won't see rain on your trip, but prior experience with hiking in such conditions can come in handy. It will be warmer in the jungle areas, and the humidity will be higher.

You may also interact with other climbers on the trail, and most people enjoy sharing their experiences. Porters will probably be coming down, and you may often be greeted with a friendly cry of "Jambo!" Later, you will break out into huge plains with little vegetation and large expanses of open country. It's quite windy there, with little cover from the elements until you reach camp. If you have the opportunity to find hikes of this type that are dry, windy, and dusty where you live, do them ahead of time.

Most visitors find bathroom facilities on Kilimanjaro to be primitive at best. There will not be toilets as you know them once you are past the gates to the park. You will, at most, have access to a hole in the bottom of a drafty outhouse with two boards on the side for your feet. This is sometimes called a "long drop" toilet. Some people do not have a good aim, and some are not feeling well, so there may be a broom in the outhouse for you to use. You will provide your own toilet paper. It's a good idea to bring wipes and sanitizing products like Purell. You will be glad you did!

You should also think about what types of food you might like when you are very tired, and (even more important) snacks that you might be able to eat at higher altitudes, where your appetite will decrease. Eating is vital for keeping up your strength, and on some days you might not feel like eating at all. It's OK to feel this way, but you will need to eat some food to maintain your mental and physical strength. Snacks between meals can be a big help.

When you imagine your climb, think of it in stages, and don't focus on the whole mountain all at once. Each day, you will go from one camp to the next. That is all you need to focus on. When you are tired, do not think of what the next day will bring: it is still far away. Just focus on this day and the task at hand. Although you might look at the mountain from time to time, do not ponder its height or the distance to the top. It will seem too big and far away. Just consider the trail right in front of you, and the steps already behind you. You do not need to do them again. Each step behind you is like a deposit in the bank of your climb on Kilimanjaro. Keep making small deposits and you will get there!

Get used to hiking or training with a short-term goal. No one can do it all at once. Your mental preparation will be just as important as your physical training. Watching videos, reading the accounts of others on their journey here, and talking to people who have made the trip will really help.

Never forget that the only real requirement on your climb is to make it back safe and sound. The summit is great, but many climbers have a good time just from doing their best and having a great adventure. If you properly prepare and train, you will probably increase your chances of getting to the summit from 50 percent to around 90 percent, maybe even a little higher. Be patient and enjoy the journey. You will have much more fun and then find yourself on the top!

TRAVELING TO TANZANIA AND THE KILIMANJARO REGION

Typical regional aircraft for traveling around Tanzania and East Africa. They are reliable and professionally run.

Kilimanjaro International Airport (JRO) is a modern, pleasant facility that can be easily reached by large aircraft from anywhere in the world. If you embark in Europe, it will take about eight to ten hours to get here. From the U.S., it's more like ten to 12 hours just to get to your European connection, depending on where you start from, then the flight from Europe to Tanzania takes roughly another nine or ten hours. The airport here is not in a town—it's about halfway between Moshi and Arusha.

The long flights are the main reason why you'll be best served by taking a day or two in Tanzania to adjust. This is very important. Later, I'll share thoughts on interesting things to do during this period.

An important consideration when traveling to Tanzania is how much you want to pay for air service. Prices vary widely. Generally, the more stops along on the way, the cheaper the trip can be. But I urge you to think this over carefully. If adding two or three extra stops saves you a couple of hundred dollars, that may not be much of a deal in the long run. Think of how tiring air travel can be and how you want to feel when you arrive. Is saving this small amount of money worth it?

You can get direct flights into Kilimanjaro International from many places in England and other parts of Europe. Flights to Amsterdam and London from the U.S. are often non-stop from many major cities. I strongly suggest you try to get here with as few stops and plane changes as possible. This will greatly improve the chances that your luggage and equipment will arrive with you, and you will feel much better when you land.

A flight or two from Europe to JRO, or two flights from the U.S., is ideal. Some clients come here from Nairobi, and you can do that, but this probably means you'll have to take an additional one-hour flight, or an arduous five-hour journey by bus, just to get to Moshi. I have done this trip and it can be difficult, trust me.

If you can afford it, premium coach, first class, or business class lets you get some much-needed rest on the plane. (Most travelers will be flying overnight.) If you'd like extra space but don't want to pay the cost for first-class or business class, you can buy an extra seat next to you. First-class costs roughly five times more than coach. Two people buying an extra seat or two can get more space for a fraction of the cost by simply buying that extra seat or seats and sharing. You can take turns curling up and resting.

If you fly to other destinations in Tanzania, I suggest you use one of our local carriers to fly you to JRO, as opposed to using other forms of transportation. For instance, the flight from Nairobi to JRO is only one hour and it's fairly convenient. Adding a bumpy bus ride will not get you here rested and ready for your climbing adventure.

The cost of flights varies widely, depending on the time of year. The best fares are offered during the two rainy seasons. You can climb then, but as I'll explain later, I don't recommend it.

I'd also warn you to be careful about buying airfares from discount carriers. Make sure the budget airline you've booked will still exist when it comes time to travel. Some discount airlines have gone bankrupt and left thousands of travelers out in the cold. Stick with reliable and established airlines and travel consultants.

Also be aware that the costs of bringing the baggage you need on a discount carrier may be far more expensive than flying on a more established airline. Your ticket price should include these costs, so that you know the real expense of your travel up front.

Upon arriving at the airport, you'll go through Tanzanian customs. You will find this process easy, comfortable, and friendly. (You can even get your visa into Tanzania ahead of time at an embassy in your home country.) After emerging from customs, a guide service or driver should be waiting to take you to your hotel. They will also assist with your bags.

Most travelers like to bring two large, lockable, zipped-up duffel bags. They need to be durable, because the porters will carry one of them throughout your climb, with all the belongings you need for camp life packed inside. Make sure your name is prominently displayed on the sides and bottom of both bags. Use a large marker or paint for this. Suitcases are a bad idea for this trip, and your porters cannot use them on Kilimanjaro.

Although you can get public transportation or rent a car, I strongly advise lining up private transportation in advance. All good tour operators and hotels can arrange this for you, and the expense is usually included in the cost of your journey. If it isn't, then you might be booking with the wrong operator.

If you are traveling in a group, you will share the vehicle with others. If you are alone or with one other person, you might come in from the airport with someone else who's staying at your hotel. This person is probably climbing at the same time you are, and you will likely see them again on Kilimanjaro during the next week. You might also see them at the bar in your hotel at night!

Driving in Tanzania is different from your home country—we have many dirt roads—but traveling here is safe, and your driver will be experienced and should be able to speak some English. On the way to your hotel, sit back and take in the sights of the plains below Kilimanjaro as you climb up to the towns and villages on the slopes of the mountain. You will pass farms, and depending on what time of year it is, you'll see sunflowers and other crops growing in abundance.

You can ride local buses in town, and it's safe to do so, but be aware that some of our buses only leave when they are full of people. "Full" is an understatement. I mean really crammed and packed, so there's little space left. Only when a bus is full will the driver leave for the next destination. This can take quite a while. For locals, it's fine, but for travelers, this might be disconcerting as your first experience in Tanzania. I would suggest that you might be better off using private transportation. Crime against visitors is very rare here in Tanzania, but on a crowded bus, it's possible you could be targeted by a pickpocket.

If you want to try the local transportation system as an adventure, go ahead, but be forewarned. If you are planning on using it because it is all you can afford, then you are probably not ready to have a safe and successful journey to climb Kilimanjaro. You might think of saving your money until you are ready to do your adventure right.

My overall advice: spending a little more for safety, security, and peace of mind is usually a wise investment.

CHAPTER NINE

I ARRIVE IN AMERICA

I am arriving at the gate in Seattle.

After spending a long night at London Heathrow, I boarded my flight to San Francisco the next morning, for another ten-hour ride on a very large airplane. I was able to relax again, and I was given free food during the flight! When we landed in San Francisco it was dark outside, so I could not see much.

When you get off the plane, obviously, you have to go through customs to gain admittance into America. In front of me, a couple of newlyweds from France, who had come to San Francisco for their honeymoon, were told their documents weren't right and they couldn't enter. They were denied admittance and sent back home. This really scared me. If their documents were not satisfactory, how would I ever get in? I thought of having come all this way only to be sent back. It was terrible.

Then it was my turn and an official told me to come to the counter. He said he needed to see my passport and invitation letter. I wondered if he could tell I was afraid. He seemed like a very important person, and I knew he had great power over me. I gave him my documents and waited as he read them carefully. I could hardly breathe. He asked me why I was traveling for such a short time—why would I be going back in only a week? I told him I had to return to work. He seemed suspicious, but he handed back my papers and passport. When he was done, he said, "You must have been invited by some very important people."

I felt lucky, and this was a memorable moment: I had been tested and was allowed to come into America! When I left the counter and walked away, it was hard to believe this dream was actually coming true.

I took a flight to Seattle, roughly three hours on a smaller plane. It was still dark, and I was very tired. I was met there by my friends Christopher and April, and as we left the airport I saw many lights from the city. I had never even imagined lights like that. There is nothing like them anywhere in Tanzania. We drove a couple of hours to Christopher and April's home, a beautiful place set high in the mountains.

From my perspective, we were driving on the wrong side of the road all the way there! This was very scary, and it took me time

Here I am at Mt Rainier in Washington State in America.

to adjust. We drive on the opposite side in Tanzania. I had never heard of such a thing.

Later in my trip, Christopher let me drive his car. He took a picture of me driving—on what I think of as the wrong side of the road—so I could share it with people back home. I have never driven on such smooth roads.

Everything in America is really big. The cars, the buildings, all the infrastructure, and even the portions of food. There were so many things that I could never have imagined before coming here. We stopped by a restaurant and I used a beautiful washroom with a TV in it. How could this be?

One night early in the trip, we drove into Seattle, a huge and beautiful city. I could not imagine how a place like this could be

I visited the Space Needle in Seattle at night. This is a very high place!

built by people. There were many lanes of cars all going in the same direction, and then there would be a flyover—what Americans call an overpass—with cars and trucks going over you in another direction! I asked Christopher to stop the car and he did. I took a picture on the side of the freeway. I said that no one in Tanzania would believe me without a photo of these flyovers. I knew I would need proof.

In Seattle, they took me to the Space Needle. Oh, my God! I was so scared when we got in the elevator. It didn't take long to get to the top, but I could not look down at all on the way up. There is glass and you can look outside and see the ground below. It is terrifying. At the top, I did not want to go to the edge because it was so far to the ground. After looking at the view, we went inside to a restaurant. As we sat and ate our food, the restaurant actually goes around in a circle, so you can see the whole city and the ocean—and the large boats that were on it.

We also went to the Seattle Aquarium and the Zoo. The zoo was scary, because you can see the tigers and even the crazy polar bears through the glass. I will never forget this. Then, while we stood there, a guy went out to feed the tigers. This seemed very dangerous to me and I will never forget that, either. When we were at the aquarium, we went under the water and saw sharks and various fish. When I got back home, almost no one could believe me about going under the water like this. Of all the things I described from my trip, this was the hardest for people to understand. This part of the aquarium where we walked was under glass, and the water was above us.

During other trips, we visited REI, the famous outdoor gear store that was founded decades ago in Seattle. They carry an amazing amount of high-quality climbing and trekking gear. As a mountain guide, I was amazed, and I wished I could buy everything and take it all back home. In Tanzania, we know stores like this exist in the U.S., but this store was like nothing I had ever seen in my life.

One day we traveled to the south side of Mount Rainier and visited the offices of IMG and RMI, which are in Ashford, Washington. This visit was very special to me, because I have worked with both companies many times when they've come to Tanzania with their clients. I got to see the guides I have met before in Tanzania! We have talked to each other on Kilimanjaro! This was one of the highlights of my trip.

We also did some hiking on Rainier, a beautiful mountain with a lot of snow on top. Even in the forests, it is cold there compared to the jungles of Kilimanjaro. But it is also beautiful. We saw many birds, animals, and plants that I have never seen before,

Dinner with Phil & Sue Ershler and friends in Seattle!

including huge Douglas fir trees. We hiked to the Freemont Lookout as evening came on, and far in the distance I could see lights from the cities below. This reminded me of looking at the lights from Kilimanjaro, but there are a lot more of them here!

Another night we went out to dinner near the ocean in Seattle, at a nice restaurant called Anthony's Pier 66. We met up with Phil and Sue Ershler. Phil is famous in Tanzania, because he's been taking American clients there for many years. Most of the top guides and operators know him, especially at the Keys Hotel. People also like him simply because he is a very nice person, friendly to everybody and respectful of our culture. When I went home, I told people at the Keys that I'd had dinner with Phil in the U.S. At first they didn't believe me, but when I showed them pictures, they did. This made me famous in my hometown.

No matter what you might think of coming on your own journey to my home here in East Africa, you won't be any more surprised or unprepared for what you see than I was. We will get back to this story later, but for now let's get back to getting you properly prepared for your trip to Tanzania and Kilimanjaro.

CHAPTER TEN

GREETING PEOPLE IN TANZANIA

Visiting in the streets with kids in Moshi Town. People are very friendly!

Introductions are important in Tanzania. My name, Kivelege, is an African clan name. Most guides will have a Western or Christian first name, but they also have a local name as well. My first name is Erick, but when I go to my village, people call me Riuwaichi, which roughly means "God knows." At a bar in town, my friends call me Erick, but they use my Chagga first name in the villages. Older people might just call me Kivelege or Mr. Kivelege. *Bwana* is formal and is used before the last name to show respect. It simply means "mister."

Most of the time around Kilimanjaro and Moshi, visitors and guests are informal with each other, and they will use your first name. At a more important event or ceremony, one might say Bwana Kivelege to show respect, or to introduce me in a more formal way. With guests, we are fine using informal greetings, in part because it makes visitors more comfortable. But I want you to be familiar with the various options when you visit. I'll say it again: introductions are *very* important in Tanzania. Being thoughtful and kind, and properly introducing yourself, will go a long way toward developing relationships and friendships. People in Tanzania are very polite.

If you walk up to a person on the street in Moshi and need directions, you will find it best to introduce yourself first, and then try to learn a little about the person you just met. Where are they from, and do they have family in the area? It does not take long to do this, and you'll see that the Tanzanian people, once properly introduced, are kind, friendly, and very warm. They will be pleased to talk to you as a visitor.

It is also considered polite to ask whether it's all right to ask a question before actually asking it. This will probably be new to you. Most people will do their best to help you, once properly introduced. Not everyone will speak your language, but many people here speak some English, and there is usually someone around who knows the language and can help. Some of the younger people may want to get to know you and will take you around town to show you the sights, often just to practice their English on you!

Swahili to English Phrases

Hello	Jambo
How are you?	Habari
Good	Nzuri
Fine	Salama
Really good	Hakuna Matata (no worries)
Good night	Lala Salama
Please	Tafadhali
Thank you	Asante
Thanks very much	Asante sana
Nice to meet you	Nafurahi kukuona
No thanks	Hapana asante
Welcome	Karibu
Goodbye	Kwa heri
You are welcome	Karibu sana
Yes	Ndiyo
No	Hapana
Excuse me	Samahari
What's your name?	Jina lakonai
I am looking for	Natafuta . . .
See you later!	Tutaonana

When you come here, you may decide to walk around Moshi and enjoy the sights. This is fine, but be aware that taking photos of government buildings is strictly prohibited.

It is considered very rude to just walk up and take someone's photo on the streets without asking. It's best to ask permission before you take anyone's photo. Most will appreciate that you asked and will likely say yes. Tanzanians really respect visitors who are polite when they visit. Manners are an important part of our culture. You might be surprised how warm and kind Tanzanians are once you get to know them. Tourists are highly valued, because they are a big help to our local economy, but it is good to understand and respect the local culture and know how to communicate with people.

It is very warm here in Moshi and Arusha, probably a lot warmer than where you are from. This may prompt you to think of wearing much lighter and more open clothes, but there are two things to keep in mind. The first is malaria. Covering your body with long sleeves and pants that are properly treated is something you should consider doing, along with using bug spray. The clothes can be lightweight, but you will need protection from both bugs and the intense sun. The second is a cultural consideration: we are a modest people. We appreciate clothes that are not too revealing, especially clothes worn by women. We do not mean to judge other people or cultures, but we respectfully ask that you consider our cultural ways when you are here. It will help you on your journey.

When you hire a guide, cook, and porters for your climb—a requirement before you can enter the park—you will enjoy the trip more if you understand a little about who these people are. Most local guides, like me, come from the Chagga tribe. Throughout this book, I will share some of my own Chagga stories so you can understand others when you travel here.

As I've mentioned, you might also want to consider learning a few simple words and phrases in Swahili. Everyone really appreciates this, and this knowledge will be of great assistance to you. You can bring a small, laminated card to refer to while you're learning. You can find some of the most commonly used words and phrases in this book. They are really pretty simple to learn and you don't need that many.

HOTELS IN MOSHI & ARUSHA

The old Keys Hotel in Moshi Town. A favorite of climbers for many years.

There are excellent first-class hotels in the Moshi area, and some are quite expensive—for higher-end places, expect to pay $200 USD per night or more. You can also find a room for as little as $11 a night, but hotels like that can seem too rustic for many travelers from Europe and the U.S. There are several good, safe places in Moshi that cost less than $100 a night. On safaris, the hotels are sometimes *very* luxurious—$500 and up—but you really don't need to spend that much. Generally, hotel costs are factored into the price of either a climb or safari, or into a package that includes both.

I'm not in the business of recommending specific hotels, so I'll just give you the basics. When looking at these facilities, online searching is particularly helpful, but, as always, don't believe everything you see and read. (I'm including photos of a few types of hotels to give you a sense of what typical places might look like.) Most guidebooks will suggest certain hotels over others, but such recommendations can't factor in your specific needs and expectations. I am confident that there is a better way to find what you need, and it is similar to finding a good guide service. In your research, talk to others from your area who have been to Tanzania. But remember that reviews from others do not mean a lot if they had vastly different expectations than you do.

When booking your trip, remember that if you use a guiding service from your own country, they will arrange all your accommodations, including your hotel stays for the entire trip, and they will be responsible for your happiness while traveling. They will also be accountable to you if you were not pleased. This can be a benefit of booking this type of package. Most established Western and European all-inclusive guide services who have been around for a while will provide lodging that meets or exceeds the needs of the average person. Some specifically cater to people who want a more rustic experience, while others will offer more modern accommodations—either way, they will make this clear to prospective clients. When booking this way, you will not even know the nightly cost of the hotel in most cases.

Traditional beehive hut style hotel in the Serengeti. It is very modern inside.

If you search on your own, feel confident that the Moshi-based hotels are safe for tourists, but be sure to check out some of the places in the more rural areas. On the way up to Kilimanjaro National Park at the Machame Gate, for example, you'll find lodging about a half hour on foot from the one of the park's main entrances. There's also a hotel close to Marangu Gate.

In Moshi, the Parkview has a reputation as one of the nicest and more expensive hotels in the region, but the prices—starting at around $64 USD per night—aren't really all that high by Western standards. (You get a lot for your money: many of the best hotels have swimming pools, and your food will be often included in the cost.) The Keys is another first-class hotel in Moshi, and there are two of them now: the original Keys, an older East African-style hotel, and the new Keys, which has 15 rooms and 15 African-style huts.

They're about two kilometers apart, and both are very climber-friendly. The new Keys is beautiful and modern. The older Keys is a bit like going back in time—it's reminiscent of the old days of big game hunting—and being there is a classic experience. It all depends on what you're looking for. I like them both and so do clients. The Keys Hotels are famous for booking climbs on Kilimanjaro, and they, along with a number of hotels in the area, specialize in catering to climbers.

There's an Impala Hotel in Moshi and also one in Arusha. The Impala in Moshi is smaller, but it's part of the same company and it's a fine place. Another beautiful property, one of the best, is the Salinero. It's in a quiet area in northwest Moshi, so it's a good choice if you prefer solitude to the more hectic pace of the town shopping area. Near the central bus station, you'll find the Parkview Inn and Bristol Cottages. This part of Moshi can be crowded and noisy, but you'll be in the middle of everything, and there are many exciting things close by to see and do.

Think of it this way: do you want to see monkeys in trees, or be close to stores and restaurants?

On the way to Marangu Gate from Moshi, you'll see the Honey Badger. This is a nice location, and you can either stay in their spacious lodge, which has 14 en-suite rooms, or you can camp on the hotel grounds. The wildlife and scenery is good here—you're likely to see monkeys and breathtaking views of Kilimanjaro. Like many hotels in the area, the Honey Badger features a large swimming pool, laundry service, a well-stocked bar, and international cuisine. And it boasts the best pizza in Moshi. This is an option that offers everything from rustic to modern accommodations. It is about six kilometers from downtown Moshi.

The Buffalo Hotel is right in the heart of Moshi. This is a good choice for locals, but I would not recommend it to clients because it will seem extremely basic by Western standards. The

Ngorongoro area hotel.

Venus Hotel is popular with backpackers; staying there is a communal, affordable experience that attracts students from many other countries. There is nothing wrong with these locations, but most climbers will find them to be less comfortable and private than they might want.

The Leopard Hotel is also right in the center of Moshi. This is a little lower-end place—rooms cost only $45 a night—but it too is popular with travelers who are on a budget.

A few other places worth checking out: the Babylon Inn, a small hotel in Marangu that sits in a beautiful mountain setting; a high-end resort called the Arumeru River Lodge ($250 a night), which is a bit far from the climbing areas; and Kili Wonders, a new and increasingly popular hotel that is very near Moshi. Over

Lake Manyara National Park area hotel.

the years, I've guided most often out of the old and new Keys Hotels, but Kili Wonders is probably my number two location these days.

Almost all these hotels will organize climbs for you, but you can also simply go to a hotel lobby and hire guides on the spot. The hotel's staff will then organize your porters and cooks.

The day before your climb starts, you'll get a briefing from your guides, in a room or designated outdoor area provided by the hotel. The next morning, the guides will come pick you up, and after that you're off. You'll take gear for the climb in one of your two duffels, which a porter will carry. The other stays at the hotel, safely locked up. The hotels manage this system well.

Overall, I would say that it's best to stay in the general Moshi/

Kilimanjaro area if you're going to climb the mountain. It's a short drive to get to the gates from this location. It's also easier for the guides to come in and make sure you're briefed properly.

You can pay as little as $11 USD a night for a room in Moshi, or as much as $1,800 USD a night for an upscale place like the Ngurdoto Mountain Lodge—in short, there is something for everyone. Safe and comfortable accommodations for climbing clients should cost you between $40 and $100 USD per night (in June 2021 dollars), and that figure ought to include excellent food and transportation.

In the end, I am not recommending any specific hotel or property, but just wanted to let you know a little about the hotels that are available. The area is safe and most of the hotels are in the business of supporting the climbing industry, so they will know it very well.

CHAPTER TWELVE

YOUR PRE-CLIMB BRIEFING

Getting to know your guides along the trail on the upper slopes of Kilimanjaro.

Before you start your climb, it's important that your guide meet with you for a briefing, a critical meeting that has to take place to ensure a safe and successful climb. They will explain the nature of the trip and answer all your questions. This process is essential.

During this process, the guides will go through all your equipment to make sure you have the proper gear. You do not want to go up the mountain and find that you're missing a piece of gear or clothing that's crucial to your safety and success. Good guides will check each item in your pack, telling you what you should leave behind and what you're missing. This process takes about an hour.

The biggest concern clients mention at these briefings is altitude—how to prepare for it and what to do if health problems develop at higher elevations. They're smart to ask about it, and we spend a lot of time on the subject. Another topic that inevitably comes up a lot: summit day. Climbers have specific questions and fears about what this will be like. People also ask about the distance we'll travel each day, handling the cold, and food.

Going through all this is a useful process. We explain that we've been up the mountain many times and know all the steps. This makes people feel much better and more confident. Confidence is critically important for a successful climb, and the briefing builds trust and an understanding of what will happen, and generates confidence in the services we provide.

Sometimes we encounter clients who clearly did not prepare properly for the trip. When they get to Moshi, they look up, see the top of Kilimanjaro from town, and suddenly realize that this climb will be much more difficult than they ever thought. It's not just a walk in the park. It is *very* difficult.

We've had people who realized right then that they were unprepared. We tell them they can try to climb Kilimanjaro if they would like, and that we will help them, and that we will make sure they're safe. Sometimes people will decide to do a portion of the climb instead of the whole thing. This is fine; they can have a great time doing this and go home very satisfied. I don't quite know how people can come so far and be unprepared, but once in a while they do. Figuring that out sooner rather than later is in everybody's best interest.

In a later chapter, I give a list of gear recommendations for each climber. At the briefing, guides will check everything you intend to take in your big duffel and in your daypack. Once your gear is set, you can't add things later, including heavy items like bottles of alcohol. On the first day of the climb, we weigh the bags before loading them onto a vehicle. The limit is strictly controlled by the National Park Service—no more than 20 kilograms each— to protect the health and safety of the porters. After the duffel is loaded, you won't see it again until the end of the first day. You'll carry your own day pack.

Carefully consider what you really need on your climb, and the weight of each item. Lightweight gear may cost a little more, but using it can really make a huge difference and creates room for other things you may want to take along. The weight of sleeping bags and pads can vary a great deal. If you pare back on weight there, you can add interesting items for your own enjoyment, or for sharing with the porters and others.

If for some reason you demand to exceed the weight limitations, we need to know ahead of time so we can arrange for an extra porter. This will involve additional cost. Under no circumstances will you be allowed to exceed the safe weight limits for what an individual porter can carry. This is a rule set by the Park Service. We weigh bags all along the route, usually each day.

We sometimes have big problems with people who try to bring things they don't need or shouldn't have. One time, I had a client who brought a huge knife. I told him it was too large and there was no need for it. He told me it was important for him to bring the knife so he could have his picture taken with it on the summit of Kilimanjaro.

Sometimes clients come up with strange ideas like this, but the answer on this request had to be no: we never allow clients to carry weapons on the mountain. About 12 years ago, I had a guy who brought a Beretta handgun. This is illegal in Tanzania, and I honestly don't know how he got it into the country. He said he accidentally brought it, but I doubt this was true.

I've seen people try to bring a lot of books, including some very large ones. I tell them they're going to be way too tired to read many books on the mountain! A guidebook can be a good idea, but large books are far too heavy to carry. A notebook can be worthwhile; most people will keep a journal, and you will probably enjoy reading what you wrote at higher altitudes when your brain was getting less oxygen. It can be very funny later!

This is also the last time we will have a chance to see if you are missing some critical piece of equipment. The good news is that there is still time to rent or buy that item in Moshi and take it along, but usually what happens is the opposite: people bring too much stuff and we make them leave things behind.

By the time your briefing is done, you will be ready to take the rest of the day off and think over everything you have learned. This is a great time to meet other climbers at your hotel. You will also very likely meet people who have just returned from a climb. You will notice them right away because of their sun-tanned faces and ear-to-ear smiles. They may have been drinking Kilimanjaro beer in celebration, and you will see them in small groups, toasting their success.

Talk to these folks about their climb. They will enjoy sharing their experiences with you, and they will tell that, although they had fears and difficulties, they made it. And if they could do it, so can you!

As you'll learn during your briefing, everything that happens on Kilimanjaro is done under the watch of National Park Service

Rangers. Working for the government of Tanzania as a ranger is a good job, in part because they get a regular, dependable monthly salary that comes to around $700 USD a month. They also get a per diem for incidental expenses. The rangers are armed—they carry AK-47s. Do not be alarmed by this, since they're doing it for your safety. These weapons are available in case there is an incident with an aggressive wild animal or a poacher, even though either problem is very uncommon these days.

In comparison, guides are almost always on contract, and we get paid for each trip—about $200 per climb, and we usually do two or three a month. However, a guide may have no clients at all in some months, depending on the time of year and prevailing weather conditions.

Rangering is a tough job. They only have five days off per month, so they'll work on the mountain about 25 days. Obviously, that's a long time away from home, and since most rangers are married, they don't like being absent from home this much. They spend a lot of time outside, they have to carry a gun, and they get lonely. Sometimes, rangers' families will camp out lower on the mountain, so the rangers can see them when they come down from higher altitudes. This is inconvenient, but people decide to make the sacrifices: it's a steady and important job.

Most camps on Kilimanjaro will have at least three Park Rangers stationed there at night, and these numbers are augmented by people who are there to do rescue work, if that proves necessary. Each rescue team usually contains four people; they work for the Park Service, but they are not rangers. You'll also see people who do camp cleaning and provide private security. All in all, there's usually a pretty big presence of Park Service people at the camps, numbering around ten or so. You will not generally see them, but it is good to know that they are there to help and protect you.

I know the rangers very well, and when they do get a day off, they like to come down to Moshi, to go out and have a beer and eat barbecue with their friends. When we see rangers on the mountain, they might say, "I'm going to be down off the mountain in two days", and of course they're looking forward to the break. I know all of them by name, which helps because we communicate with them frequently on the radio.

Our radios allow us to call ahead and find out which rangers will be in charge at the next camps. Our good working relationship with the Park Rangers is critical to your safety, especially if you need medical attention, or in case you have to be evacuated. They are professional and well-trained. We are very proud of them and the work they do.

CHAPTER THIRTEEN

RELAXING IN MOSHI BEFORE YOUR CLIMB

Mweka Village area on the slopes of Kilimanjaro. These are great places to visit and have a fun and relaxing day!

When you arrive in Tanzania, you will be tired from your travels, and you may have significant jet lag. The country is new to you and so is our climate, which is very close to the equator. Even in Moshi, which is higher than the coastal cities, it is usually in the low 80's to low 90's each day (although it cools down very nicely at night to the 60's). So it's time to take a break and get to know the place while you get ready for your climb.

Because I've traveled to England and America, I know exactly how it feels to go so far and adjust to different time zones. It can be really tough, especially for first-time travelers. I certainly wouldn't want to travel that far and start a climbing journey the very next day. It would be too much.

Unfortunately, many companies and guidebooks don't do enough to thoroughly educate people about how critical this can be. Some companies don't like to tell you that you need to spend a couple of extra days on the ground in Tanzania, because people might not want to commit to the added expense. This is a big mistake. Spending two or even three days taking it easy before you climb is important. Two days is really the minimum. You will be happier and more relaxed when you start climbing.

Without this rest period, we guides end up having a big problem, because climbers get too tired during the day and want to take a nap whenever they stop. Although it's important to climb slowly—*pole, pole*—being tired from jet lag is very different.

When you have jet lag, you will not sleep properly at night on the mountain. This problem goes away when you've spent just a few days around town getting used to being in Tanzania. Climbers should probably not even be allowed to book a trip without taking this consideration into account. There are many things to do in and around Moshi, and as you adjust your sleep habits and get used to our climate, you can also have some fun!

In fact, I have some great ideas!

Visit a School

How would you like to bring real joy to some kids and make friends for life here in Africa? Visiting a school is easy, safe, and a great way to spend part of a day.

We have many schools, so just tell your guide you want to visit one and they will set it up, usually one day in advance, with the headmaster of a local elementary school. The kids will be so happy to see you. They will have many questions about you and your homeland. You'll visit different classrooms, and the kids will enjoy singing for you. Either your guide or the teacher can do the interpreting if you need it. Most teachers will speak English.

Kids here are like kids everywhere else: eager to learn. Education is very important in Tanzania; every village has a school. Schools are the center of our local culture and we are very proud of them. Kids in government-sponsored elementary schools wear the same uniform, which helps all of them feel equal, no matter how wealthy or poor their family may be. We believe all kids deserve the same chances in their learning environment.

Science, mathematics, and language are some of the most important classes; English, history, and geography are also given a lot of attention. English is taught at all the schools, but most of the instruction happens in Swahili.

Our kids can't bring food from home, because some families are poor, and some have money. All kids eat the same food, a lot of which comes from school gardens worked by the students. By growing vegetables and flowers, the kids learn to work together as a team. Remember our national motto: Unity is the Power. No matter the tribe or background, everyone gets a chance to learn and improve themselves.

Although you do not need to bring anything or pay anything for these visits, donations of materials are always welcomed, and items like pencils and paper are much-needed. If you bring some items, just give them to the teacher and they'll pass them out. Another very welcome donation: books. Most of the people in Tanzania don't have many books. They don't get an opportunity to do a lot of reading, except for newspapers, which only have current news. Not a lot of people get to sit down and have a chance to read a novel. Books in English—in particular, what you might call exam books—are needed, for any subject that typically comes up in schools. They will all be welcome.

School visits are not something that most tour operators offer, but they're easy to set up. It works best if you have a guide with you, and there are many people who are more than willing to do this work. Either your climbing guide or the staff at any local hotel can find someone for you with ease. I am hopeful that with this book, people will rethink their trip to Tanzania and that in the future, this will be part of many new and different adventures that travelers consider when they visit my homeland.

Hang Out at a Local Bar & Have a Beer

Every community has bars. In ours, there's usually a television where people can watch soccer games while they have a beer. If you'd like to visit one, you'll be most welcome. One quick word of warning: drink beer from a bottle and don't eat the local barbecue that's often served in bars. You might get sick just in time for your climb. Locals have immunity from many things that can make you ill, and the cooking in local bars will not be up to a standard necessary for visitors. You can also go to the bars in rural villages but be careful not to get lost on the local trails if you get off the main roads. It is easy to do in these rural areas.

Be sure to sample the local Kilimanjaro beer! It's excellent!

You might consider asking your guide or someone from your hotel to go with you to a bar, since they speak the local language and can answer questions. Or you can just go by yourself, and you'll get a friendly welcome. Bar owners are happy to have tourists come in, and locals don't mind this, either. About 40 percent of the people in Tanzania speak pretty good English; most everyone knows at least a few basic phrases. Remember what I told you about taking pictures of people without their permission. If you have a local guide with you, they will make sure picture-taking is okay. Never just assume it's all right.

There is a very good beer made in Tanzania: Kilimanjaro. Safari is another brand we make. Both are premium beers manufactured in Dar es Salaam. If the beers are from a bottle, they are completely safe.

Explore Moshi and Shop

In the past, most travelers went to their hotel, ate and stayed there, climbed the mountain, and then went back home. Travelers are now doing things very differently, exploring both Moshi and outlying villages. It's helpful to have a guide when you do this, which as always can be arranged through your hotel. When you shop in Moshi, a guide can negotiate in Swahili and help you get the best deals.

The Moshi Town District area, which encompasses Moshi and the surrounding communities, is safe for tourists, and a lot of people like to simply walk around and see the sights. This is a great experience for tourists during the daytime—it's best not to go out unaccompanied at night. Although it's perfectly safe to drink beer or some other drink sealed in a bottle, you should be wary of street vendor food, and you should also avoid banana wine and banana beer, very popular drinks among locals that are not safe for visitors. I had a client whose climb was ruined after he became ill from banana wine.

There are street vendors all over the place, selling local items that will remind you of your journey to Africa. The bus station and the central market are two good places to find vendors. Remember to think ahead about shipping, especially if you buy something special like the beautiful wood carvings made here. Later in the book, you'll find more about shopping for souvenirs.

Most vendors will take both American dollars and Tanzanian shillings. If freelance sellers approach you on the street, it's OK to tell them no, even if they're persistent and follow you around. There's no reason to be alarmed by this, so you should relax and have fun. Sometimes when you first come into town, a fairly large number of adults, or a group of kids, will come up to you to see what's going on. They might even follow you around for a while, but don't worry: they are just interested in you. If this sort of attention worries you, take a guide along until you adjust. Your hotel or climbing guide can set this up for you.

Bike Around Town

Bike rentals in Moshi are about $20 a day. A guide costs about $50, and while hiring a guide isn't required by every company, it's a good idea. They know their way around and they know good places to leave your bike if you stop to do some shopping. Biking is one of the great ways to get around Tanzania and see the different towns and villages, and it's becoming very popular. Some Tanzanian guides are starting up bike tour businesses.

Mountain Biking on Kilimanjaro

On the Kenyan side of Kilimanjaro—the northern side—the National Park allows people to bike on the mountain in an area where the trail is not as steep. I personally think that biking on Kilimanjaro is not very safe, but people with the right level of skill could have a good time, if they are willing to take the risks. Medical assistance for a serious crash will not be available in Tanzania, and you will need permission from the Park Service, along with an insurance policy in case you require rescue.

Visit a Coffee Plantation

When you're driving to the gates to climb Kilimanjaro, you will notice clear signs of coffee production on the slopes. Tanzania is famous for high-quality coffee, which grows well in our volcanic soil. Coffee from the Kilimanjaro region would be similar to the famous Kona coffee from Hawaii, another place with volcanic soil.

There are coffee plantations you can visit; most are about a 45-minute drive from the downtown Moshi hotels. The cost of a tour is roughly $45, and you can buy coffee to ship home. This is a lot of fun and I strongly recommend these tours to my clients. They always seem to have a great time!

Kikuletwa Hot Spring

Not far from Moshi—about an hour drive—you'll find a very appealing waterfall and hot springs called Kikuletwa. It's also called Maji Moto, but that name can be confusing, since there are other springs with the same label. Maji Moto simply means "hot" or literally "fire" water in Swahili.

If you visit, you should enjoy the view of the spring, take a swim, and do a guided cultural tour, which you can book in advance through your hotel. These tours include a walk to a local village for lunch. If you want to be extra-safe, bring a lunch-to-go from your hotel, but you should be fine either way.

In Rundugai Village, which is part of this location, you'll see amazing baobab trees, along with native fig trees that surround the springs. There are excellent views of both Kilimanjaro and Meru, and there is no danger from animals in this area. You can also experience the local ethnic cultures on your visit and tour. You will be very welcome. There are many bird and primate species in the area as well.

Visit a Local Village

Even though I'm a guide, I can still get lost walking around some of the local villages. Once in a while, when I'm on some of the more rural trails, I have to stop and ask for directions. All of which is another way of saying: if you decide to visit a rural village, take a guide, because their presence will make everything easier.

Marangu is a fun village to visit, but there are others as well. I've been on trips where as many as 50 people from the village, including kids, started walking along with us, and it's fun. People in the villages love to share with visitors. It makes them happy. Mweka, which is the main exit from the park, is also a popular area for visitors, and there are many things to see here, including shops and local bars.

Most villagers work on farms or in some type of business associated with farming. Farming often involves caring for domestic animals like cattle and goats. Some people collect bananas. Each village has a couple of days every week in which producers bring to market what they've raised, gathered, or grown. People will come from around Tanzania and even from other countries to purchase items at these wholesale markets. They will transport their purchases by truck back to where they're needed. Buyers from Dar es Salaam or Arusha may come to a local market and purchase items there, and you can watch this happening when you visit.

The main markets are in Moshi and Arusha, but each local village has its own market area as well. It's a lot of fun to see all this activity, but remember to eat only properly prepared food or items that you peel yourself before eating them—like a banana, or better yet, a box lunch from your hotel.

Day Trip to Mount Meru and Arusha National Park

Prior to your climb, you can take half a day and visit Mount Meru in Arusha National Park, which is a short distance from Kilimanjaro, Moshi, and Arusha. This is a great way to get used to the climate and the new time zone. You'll also have a good chance of seeing wildlife.

There are far more animals around Meru than you will find on and around Kilimanjaro, including giraffes, elephants, warthogs, and buffaloes. There are no lions in this area. You will not normally have problems with animals there, but if you climb Meru, you'll have to hire someone with a gun as a safety precaution.

Mount Meru is surrounded by many small lakes that you can explore. The lakes are what make the area attractive to animals. You might see hippos here from time to time, which you'll be viewing from the safety of a vehicle.

My favorite animal in all of Africa, as I will talk more about later, is the giraffe, and you might see them here from a very close distance. To me, this is the most beautiful and graceful animal. I think that they will be pleased that you have come to see them as well!

Climbing Mount Meru

Some people like to climb Mount Meru as an acclimatization for Kilimanjaro. If you have time, and you can afford the price, this is an excellent way to increase your chances of getting to the summit of Kilimanjaro. Doing Meru takes a few days, and it's a serious effort: this peak is 4,566 meters tall, or 14,980 feet. It is considered more difficult to climb than Kilimanjaro because of several challenging trail sections near the summit. Operators are now offering longer climbs on Meru for people who want to make this their primary climb in East Africa.

It takes about two hours to get to Meru from Moshi. On the first day of climbing, you'll do only about three hours of walking. After going through Momella Gate, you start out in the forest. There are only two camps on Meru: Miriakamba Hut and Saddle Hut.

Only about 60 percent of the people who try Meru get to the top, because there's a very difficult section right near the summit.

Mount Meru from the slopes of Kilimanjaro.

Even if you don't, it's still a great trip. Kilimanjaro doesn't have any difficult sections like Meru does. There is one section near the top that is very steep and narrow. I like this climb very much, but I do not like to take clients who are not strong enough or are too worried about such steepness.

I've never had a single client fall or get injured in this area, but I know other guides who have. I spend a lot more time on Meru watching over the clients on summit day and telling them to be very careful than I ever would on Kilimanjaro.

It's actually more comfortable to do Meru in four days, but many people do it in three. You are required to have porters and a guide, since Meru is part of the National Park system. Please do not try to climb this illegally on your own, because this is against the law. Meru is under the same permit system used in all of our national parks. There are no tents allowed on the Meru climb and you will be staying in huts. It has the same system and ratio of guides and porters to clients, as well as the same weight limitations.

Near the summit, there are four sections where the Park Service has put in a chain so clients can hold on when they go through narrow and very steep sections. Guides do not use ropes here, and the clients just hold onto the chains. I do not think it is too dangerous for most people.

Generally, it costs about an extra thousand dollars to add Meru to your Kilimanjaro trip. The more you spend, the more inclusive your services will be. Making Meru your primary destination is a different story altogether, and it can be an excellent destination by itself. It's not crowded, which is one reason Meru is becoming more popular as a destination.

Not to scare you, but in 2008 I was climbing Meru with a man from England, and we had an interesting encounter with buffaloes. We had the required Park Ranger along with us, and he had a gun. We were just getting up to a big saddle when we came across a lone buffalo in the brush, and he was not happy. These animals can be ill-tempered sometimes, especially if they are alone. For some reason, this buffalo charged us, and the ranger had to shoot and kill it. The client was so frightened that he ran all the way down to the bottom of the mountain, and we could not find him for quite a while. I did not think a person could run so far so fast. I do not think anything like this will happen to you if you go Meru, but it is kind of a funny story!

CHAPTER FOURTEEN

TIPPING, BANKING, AND CASH

A guide and climber just below the rim of the crater on summit morning.

In the old days, people used to keep money in their house. Today, most people store money on their cell phone. Technology has changed everything, even in Moshi. I suspect this will surprise you. But no matter how rural and distant this land may seem to you; technology has changed things everywhere in the world.

There are few banks in the villages, and not many people use them today, because it's difficult and expensive. You have to go to town to get cash anymore, so be aware that the cash and banking system described in other books are quickly fading out. Obtaining cash from local banks will be expensive and cumbersome—and in some areas, impossible. You should plan ahead for this, because you will usually need cash on your trip.

Most people here use Tanzanian shillings. If you go to a local bar, it's a good idea to use them there as well, although everyone will generally also accept U.S. dollars too. It's also better to use shillings in local stores and villages. You can get them from your hotel or travel operator for a small fee. I would not suggest getting them from a local bank, because of high services charges.

As of this writing (June 2021), a U.S. dollar is worth roughly 2,400 shillings, but this rate fluctuates all the time. When you come here, try to have an idea of how the local exchange rate compares with what you want to pay someone, based on the exchange rate from your home country. A note we use often is for 1,000 shillings—about 43 cents USD—but there are several larger notes, too.

One other point about our local currency: some people like to take shillings home as a souvenir, but doing this is illegal and it is prohibited to take our Tanzanian currency out of the country.

Among the Tanzanian guides, American climbers and visitors are very popular because they are usually well-prepared for the trip and they are also the most courteous about tipping. Tipping is a very important part of how guides, cooks, and porters make a living, and Americans embrace this more than any other nationality. Some other countries do not follow the same tipping principles, and this becomes a hardship for the people who work on the mountain.

If you come from a country that does not embrace tipping, please try to understand this system when you travel here. People in Tanzania do not make a lot of money, and our work on Kilimanjaro is hard and seasonal. Workers who don't get tips have a difficult time supporting their families.

An appropriate tip for your porters would be roughly $10 USD per day per porter. For cooks it would be at least $15 to $20 per day, per cook. Assistant guides should get at least $20 to $25 per day. The senior guide should get at least $30 per day per client. The biggest tip I ever received from an individual client for a trip was $700. I know of a guide from another company who once got tipped $3,000 by one client for a single climb. This is a lot of money in Tanzania, and an amount like that would be shared with our family members and the entire village.

What about tipping through your hotel or guiding company? If you leave a tip this way, it's important to write down instructions—which you will give to your lead guide—about the amount that you're tipping everyone, so they can share those tips fairly. The lead guide can go to the bank, get the money, and pay his people. They do not deduct anything from your tip, and they make sure that everyone gets the full amount.

At least the reputable companies do. If a tour operator or hotel ever tried to cheat a guide, the guides would never do business with them again. This would be very bad news for them throughout the climbing community. It is not how we do business in Tanzania.

If you go to an ATM in Tanzania, you can only get Tanzanian shillings. U.S. dollars can be obtained at a bank. It's easy to do, but don't forget to bring your passport as I.D. The service charge is high—around 18 percent—so you'll be better off if you bring cash from home.

Many hotels now have ATMs that you can use with a credit card, and some companies will help you tip your guides, cooks, and porters with a credit card. (You tell them the amounts and they charge the total to your card.) Check ahead with companies to make sure they provide this service.

Sometimes clients will decide they want to send money to Tanzania after returning home, usually as an extra tip or gift. However, it's risky to send money to Tanzania by mail, because post office workers are likely to open it. They claim this is done for security reasons, but the bottom line is that if they find money in the mail, they might take it out. It's safer to use Western Union to send such funds. Another benefit to this approach: when somebody sends money through Western Union to Tanzania, the money is not taxed, so the recipient gets the full amount themselves. It is cheap to do and quite secure.

CHAPTER FIFTEEN

GEAR ESSENTIALS

Your duffle bags will look like this at camp. What should you have in them?

In the old days, if you forgot particular pieces of gear or clothing, or your luggage was lost, you had a real problem, because it wasn't possible to replace these things in Tanzania. Imagine if you got here and didn't have your boots. You can't climb very well without them!

Today this is not nearly as much of an issue, because there are many outfitters in Tanzania who rent and sell gear. In fact, you could arrive and buy or rent virtually everything you need. This is not the best way to outfit yourself—it's expensive and time-consuming—but it can be done.

Another reason people may choose to rent: they're not hardcore trekkers, and they don't plan to use the equipment after their once-in-a-lifetime climb of Kilimanjaro. And please always remember this: if you happen to bring equipment that you'll only use once, such items are always treasured by Tanzanian guides, porters, and cooks if you wish to donate them at the end of your climb.

Finally, some people simply bring the wrong gear, or they didn't realize that some things they brought from home are out of date. That flannel sleeping bag you used in the backyard as a child probably isn't going to cut it on Kilimanjaro! It's best to assess what will and won't work before you arrive.

Of all the essentials, boots are at the top of the list. Yes, you can buy them here, and they may work fine, but the wrong boots, or improperly fitting boots, can spell disaster. *Good boots are so important that you should not even put them in your checked baggage—they should be worn or carried on the plane.* Don't worry about what people think of how you look on the plane. This is too important to take chances.

And be sure to bring boots that fit and are already broken in. The way a well-used boot conforms to your feet is a delicate match, and a good fit is the best way to avoid blisters, which can scuttle a climb. Also, make sure the boots are waterproof and relatively lightweight. And remember that you don't need heavy mountaineering boots, which are generally made from plastic with wooden soles inside. That is far sturdier footwear than you need for this climb, and the weight and stiffness of such boots will end up being a hindrance.

Tulips, Wooden Shoes, Batteries, and a Torch

Before we get into more gear specifics, I want to tell you a story of a man I met from Holland in 2009, who was with another group, but got to know some of my clients on the trail. This tale illustrates the unexpected little things that can go wrong with gear, and how much they matter.

His name was Wesley Schroder, and he had trained relentlessly for Kilimanjaro by bicycling back and forth on local trails. Unfortunately, Holland sits below sea level, so he was actually doing negative altitude during all this bike riding. In addition, biking and hiking up a mountain are not the same thing—you use different muscle groups. His inappropriate training style made his climb difficult, and he suffered quite severely at times from altitude sickness. He was also mentally discouraged that his hard work hadn't prepared him for the real conditions on the mountain.

One day, not far from Horombo Camp, on the Marangu Route, Wesley stumbled into a rest area where my clients were eating and relaxing. He believed he was close to death. He was not, of course, but your perspective can change when discouragement sets in! He fell to the ground and just stayed there for a while with his pack on. My climbers—and two very kind sisters from another climbing group—helped him get his pack off, gave him water and a light lunch, and generally tried to cheer him up. Soon he felt much better.

Wesley made it the rest of the way to Horombo Camp and settled in for the night. The next day, he suffered more altitude problems and decided once again that he was dying. We were all heading up to Mawenzi Hut for the day to acclimatize, and then back down to Horombo for a second night. Wesley made it through and—once again with the support of newfound friends—regained his composure and confidence.

That night, a truly terrible disaster hit Wesley from Holland! To his horror, he turned on his torch and discovered that it was dead. (A torch is the U.K. term for what Americans call a head-lamp or flashlight.) Inside an A-frame hut where two of my clients were staying, he explained the problem. My clients, who were Americans, listened with great interest, and they became deeply concerned that Wesley had actually brought a flame-burning torch to the mountain with him, which would potentially be very dangerous. They didn't understand what he really meant.

Eventually, Wesley produced the torch and my clients saw that he was referring to a battery-powered headlamp. They real-ized he had drained all his batteries because he'd made a common mistake: he didn't know that batteries go dead faster in the cold. Batteries that had worked well in Holland were failing on the slopes of Kilimanjaro. There was some further confusion, because Wesley thought American batteries wouldn't work in a European device. But of course they do. The Americans gave him some lith-ium batteries—far better than the alkaline ones he'd brought—and his torch magically lighted up with full power. The disaster was averted.

Wesley was a considerate man, and he offered to pay for the batteries, but this is not how we do things in Tanzania. You will find that if you are broke and need a beer at a local bar, someone with the resources will buy you one. This gesture is not considered a loan—it's just the right thing to do. This is Tanzania.

In the end, Wesley dug deep within himself, and on the final day, after getting so much support and encouragement from oth-ers, he found the strength to get to the top of Uhuru Peak! After he returned to Holland, he sent a pair of wooden shoes and some tulips to my clients, in recognition of their kindness and help. If you can imagine a gesture like this, you will be well on your way to thinking like a Tanzanian!

Gear for Your Trip

For about $2 to $4 USD, you can buy a sim card for your cell phone, which will work in Tanzania. I would encourage you to have a cell phone, but to spend less time using it when you're here. You should not travel all the way to Africa just to look at your phone all the time.

When choosing the clothes that you'll bring, remember that you'll be hiking in many different environments. Early on, there will be subtropical jungles with monkeys in the trees; later, you'll be hiking and sleeping not far from glaciers, and on some nights (not often) you'll be sleeping on snow! Think of bringing many layers, which will allow you to wear as much or as little clothing as you need each day. You should bring lighter-weight layers that fully cover your arms and legs; made from material that can protect you from bug bites while keeping you comfortable. You'll also need layers of shirts, light jackets, and warmer jackets, along with an outer layer that is wind-proof for cold, blustery days up high.

Your clothes should be highly breathable, synthetic, and have moisture-wicking properties. Such clothing is easy to find at all outdoor supply stores, and it is far better than wool. Cotton should be avoided entirely because of its weight and sogginess.

Buying the proper socks is critical: bring at least two pairs of heavy socks—this is the one place for wool—with light synthetic liners. This combination will probably smell bad before the trip is over, but it will protect your feet. You can freshen up the socks and liners on the trail by laying them out on a rock in direct sunlight.

The intense radiant heat will kill microbes, while the fresh air and sunshine will air out the material.

A down climbing jacket is great to have if you can afford one, and it's possible to buy them used or to rent them. For example, Rainier Mountaineering, one of the prominent American guiding companies in Washington State that I've mentioned, sells many single-use jackets at the end of the climbing season. They come from climbers who bought them solely to take on Rainier, then no longer wanted them.

Either way, make sure to get a size that will fit over all your other clothes. (These big jackets are also good as a second layer over your sleeping bag on very cold nights.) When you're not using them, these jackets are remarkably light and can be rolled up to fit into a very small stuff sack. Even the super-warm Eddie Bauer Peak XV Down Jacket, which is rated to minus 35 degrees Fahrenheit, weighs just over two pounds.

Bring some thermal underwear, and make sure the fit is not too tight, since this lessens their effectiveness as a thermal layer. As usual, the materials should be synthetics that wick, not cotton.

Your best defense against high winds is an outer shell, or an oversized rain jacket with a good hood. This jacket must be large enough to fit over everything you will be wearing on summit day, including your big down jacket. Remember that your jacket will puff up when you have it on, so the larger your outer shell, the better. Prior to coming to Tanzania, put on everything you would possibly wear on a cold day, including a hat, and make sure the outer layer fits comfortably over all of it.

When it comes to gloves, again, layers work well. A light-weight pair, with sturdy larger gloves that can go over them, is the best combination, and there are many types of materials to choose from these days. It would be wise to bring a pair of heavy-duty mittens for summit day, just in case it's very windy. These will allow your fingers to be pressed together and warm up, even if you only do this briefly before putting standard gloves back on. An extra pair of gloves is always a good idea, in case you lose one glove along the way.

You will need two hats, maybe three. Definitely bring a large-brim sun hat with a chin strap. You'll also need a wool hat for cold nights and summit day; it should completely cover your head and ears. A baseball cap is nice for hanging around camp after a day of trekking.

You'll need a sleeping bag, regardless of whether you're in a tent or in a hut, and you'll want to choose down, because it is the warmest. Down bags are lightweight, and they stuff down to a very small size. If you're sleeping with someone else, you can convert the bags into a single bag that holds two people. You just unzip them and then zip them back together into a single large bag. This system can provide incredible warmth on cold nights.

Some guidebooks will tell you to skip bringing a sleeping mat or pad. This is bad advice. If you are in a hut, you'll be sleeping on plywood. If you think this might feel OK since you'll be inside a sleeping bag, put your bag on the concrete floor of a garage and see how that feels for a night. Inflatable sleeping pads are fairly lightweight and easy to bring along, so don't skimp on comfort. Another good idea is an additional pad: the ones made using egg carton-style foam are great. Using these with an inflatable one is very comfortable, and they are lightweight.

You don't need to bring a tent, because they should always be provided as part of your package, and porters will set them up ahead of your arrival at camp each night.

Definitely bring trekking poles—they help with both your stamina and stability. Do not bring ski poles. They are not the same and they do not collapse down properly for packing. Instead, buy lightweight carbon fiber poles that can be retracted easily when you're not using them, or when you're traveling. Practice using them prior to coming; they'll seem like second nature by the time you get here.

I would bring two headlamps, just in case, because you'll be stymied if you don't have a working headlamp on summit day. They are lightweight, not very expensive, and they run on small batteries. You are required to have an extra set of batteries when you begin your final summit approach, so bring spares. Take them home or donate them when the climb is over.

Sunscreen and sunglasses are critical. You can get severely burned by sun and radiation at high altitude, so you'll need a minimum SPC of 30, but 60 is better. Bring lip balm that has a high SPF as well, at least 30.

Sunglasses are a necessity, too, because you can't deal with high-altitude sun and radiation without them. I recommend so-called glacier glasses, which feature small cups around the lens frame to block out sunlight from the sides. Also bring a second set of polarized sunglasses in a hard case, as a backup. You can't climb without protecting your eyes against the sun. If you drop your only pair and someone steps on them, you will not be able to continue your climb safely.

Bring earplugs for windy nights in a tent, or just to block out noise around the camp. Some people will be coughing at night as they adjust to the altitude, and this can keep you from sleeping. Feel free to bring along an iPod, or something like it, but don't use these devices on the trail on summit morning: you need to be able to hear your guides. Some people bring audio books or a journal; both are relatively lightweight and a good idea.

You'll need a day pack as you hike up the mountain, with plenty of pockets and sufficient volume to hold all the things you'll need during the day. You'll also need water bottles—I think four per person is about right, made of BPA-free Nalgene, holding about a quart or liter each. On summit days, you'll need a couple of insulating covers or your bottles will freeze. If your water freezes on summit day and you don't have anything to drink, you may not make it to the top. This would be a silly and completely avoidable reason to fail.

Bring heavy duty plastic bags for all your items so they don't get wet when it rains. Always pack everything in plastic bags each day, even the items that your porters will carry. Your day pack should have a plastic bag as a liner on the inside to keep everything dry and usable. If your gear gets wet, you will have a tough time getting it dry again.

Pack and bring along daily snacks for the trail. Maybe bring a few extra items for a midnight snack, for times when you can't sleep, or for visiting in your tent at night with others. Some people like to bring their own instant coffee or tea. The cooks or porters will provide you with coffee and tea, or hot water each morning, or in evening time if you wish, to use for brewing.

When creating your final list, remember to go back and review the upcoming chapter on water and water purification systems. Remember to bring multiple systems for your safety. Do not put any untreated water into your body, or you could become very sick and ruin your entire trip.

As I've said, you don't need maps or a compass or anything like that—the guides will handle route-finding. If you want to bring maps, a compass and a GPS for fun, feel free to bring them, but they are not necessary. Please do not use them as a reason to debate with your guides, because they will always know where they are at all times.

This list is not exhaustive, because everyone is different, but it should be a fairly good guide as you begin your planning. Talk to others who have come here and see what they think. Bring everything you need, but nothing more than is necessary. Sometimes

Basic Equipment Checklist

Boots – proper fitting and broken in!
Trekking poles (not ski poles) that collapse when not in use
2 large lockable duffel bags
2 headlamps (torches)
At least 4 sets of lithium batteries for each
2 to 4 sets of wool hiking socks
2 to 4 sets of thin sock liners – silk is best
Thermal underwear
Synthetic climbing pants
Two long sleeve climbing shirts
Large brim sun hat with chin strap
Wool hat for summit day and sleeping
Baseball cap for camp
Light jacket – synthetic
Medium jacket - synthetic
Down or similar cold weather jacket
Large waterproof outer shell jacket with hood
Sleeping bag – down is best – low temp rated
Inflatable air mattress (& foam one too if you want)
Glacier glasses & extra pair of polarized sunglasses
Cold weather gloves and lighter ones for inside them (pair of mittens is good too)
Sunscreen & lip balm (all high SPF and test ahead of time for reaction to skin)
4 one quart/liter Nalgene water bottles (& 2 insulated covers for summit day)
Water purification systems (at least two, or even three) Iodine/Filter/Steripen
Heavy duty plastic bags for all items when traveling to protect from rain/moisture
Ziplock bags for personal items and trash
Snacks for the trail each day or for the evening, or to share with people
Toilet paper, personal wipes, Purell, mask, toiletry items, medications & Rxes
Journal and pens that write in very cold/freezing weather, iPod, music, guidebook
Manual camera and several rolls of film in case electronic one fails in the cold
Extra copies of all travel documents, passport, visa, medical prescriptions, etc.

people do not bring enough for the climb, but it is far more likely that they bring too much. We will sort this out at your briefing. You can email pictures of your entire setup in advance, and we can look it over with you ahead of time.

And please, please do not bring a weapon. Do not bring alcohol to celebrate your summit day. Plan on taking everything back down off the mountain when you leave.

Dirt

Many people will tell you that they have never been so dirty as when they came down from Kilimanjaro. The mountain is a volcano, and there is always fine volcanic dust around. The wind blows and the dust goes everywhere, finding its way into every crack and crevice of your gear, clothing, and body.

You should bring a face scarf for days when the dust is bad. An N95 mask will work great, but you would need a few of them, because they tend to get dirty and plug up. This is not necessary on the lower parts of the climb, but it can be on the last couple of days up high.

One issue that crops up in groups is that one or two climbers always seem to kick up dust by dragging their feet. Don't offend them by telling them how to walk. Instead, make sure there's enough space between trekkers so that dust is less of a problem.

Don't even think of trying to keep from being dirty, staying clean, or not smelling bad—it's not possible. However, you can keep yourself feeling cleaner by bringing some baby wipes. These can be a lifesaver for your tentmates or fellow climbers, making it easy to clean up some of your personal areas from time to time. Don't throw them away on the mountain: bring a plastic bag and pack them out. On some routes, you will get some soap and a basin of water. These are really great, but they are not the same as a bath—trust me on this.

Important Documents

Always bring a separate photocopy of your important travel documents, like insurance, itinerary, passport, and visa. Keep them in a separate place from the originals, in case they get lost or stolen. Your embassy can help in replacing them if you have these copies.

CHAPTER SIXTEEN

WHEN TO SCHEDULE YOUR TRIP

Evening time at a camp just after leaving the jungle on the Machame Route.

Today is April 17, 2021, and it's still raining really hard. It's too much. Yes, rain is good for farmers, because they will use the water and sediment to grow new crops, but right now there's mud everywhere. This makes it very difficult to get around town, because the volcanic soil we have is quite slippery. It's hard to explain how much water and mud is flowing by my house right now; many people are forced to stay inside their homes. You should seriously think about these weather conditions when planning your trip. Very soon the rains will suddenly end, and the long dry season will be underway once more!

However, right now, we're in what's known as the long rainy season, which runs from early March to early May. The short rainy season takes up all of November and the first half of December. Some people choose to climb Kilimanjaro and tour Tanzania during the long rainy season, but not many. More people come during the short rainy season than the long one. It does not last very long and there is nowhere near as much rain each day.

You can get great deals to climb Kilimanjaro during these wet times, but in reality, climbing is either impossible or very unpleasant. Keep that in mind when shopping for bargains. You will certainly get what you pay for in the rainy seasons, and you might need a life jacket!

Although it can rain all day during these periods, it's usually wettest at night and around noon. Rain falls all the way up the mountain, turning to snow above 3,500 meters (around 12,000 feet), making Kilimanjaro white on top. To give you the idea: there's an average of 15 inches of rain on the mountain in April. That equates to roughly 15 feet of snow at higher elevations. This is where the famous glaciers came from.

As I've said, during the rainy season, guiding costs are lower, which is why some clients decide to climb then. But please be aware of the pitfalls, which will color your experience. You have to carry quite a bit more personal gear each day, because it's difficult to dry things out when it's so generally wet. It's also difficult to get

JAN	FEB	MAR	APR	MAY	JUN	JUL	AUG	SEP	OCT	NOV	DEC
78ᶠ	78ᶠ	77ᶠ	76ᶠ	72ᶠ	70ᶠ	69ᶠ	70ᶠ	71ᶠ	75ᶠ	76ᶠ	77ᶠ
25°	25°	25°	24°	22°	21°	20°	21°	21°	23°	24°	25°

dry at night, so you and your gear will be damp most of the time. Even the porters, who are very tough, don't like it.

Deep water will make many crossings extremely slippery and muddy. It's difficult to go anywhere in the jungle areas at these times. As you get higher on the mountain, it won't bother you as much, but there will be a lot of water running down the trails during the heavy rainy season. There's not much wind with the rain, but it's a heavy rain.

Another consideration during the rainy season is that on a few really bad days, it's difficult to even get to the mountain gates. The drive from Moshi can be difficult and some roads and crossings can become unpassable, or at least very unsafe, causing you delays on your trip. These delays can also occur on the mountain itself, causing difficulties with your itinerary.

Late May, June, July, August, September, and October are by far the best months to climb Kilimanjaro. Another good window starts in the middle of December and runs through January and February and into March. July, August, September, and January—and sometimes into February—are the driest months, and you will not see much rain at all during any of them. You could easily spend two or three weeks in Tanzania, climbing Kilimanjaro and going on a safari, and see little if any rain during your entire trip.

Fires used to be a big problem during the dry season, but now that the Park Service keeps wildlife poachers out of Kilimanjaro—poachers were once a major nuisance, but they're very uncommon these days—and now that guides are required to be much more cautious when heating and cooking food, the fire danger has been reduced. You will sometimes see fires in the national parks during these times, but these are controlled burns—usually occurring in the grasslands of the lower parks—and they won't affect your trip.

CHAPTER SEVENTEEN

LEARNING THE HISTORY AND GOVERNMENT IN AMERICA

Me at the Legislature in Washington State.

It's now time to return to my trip to America, and how life-changing it was for me. I wanted to understand more about the culture and history of the U.S., and my friends thought of various fun and interesting ways for this to happen. One day they took me to a movie at the Boeing IMAX Theater in Seattle. I had never been to a movie in a theater before this. They gave me special glasses, and with those on, everything changed: it seemed like I was in the movie myself, as if I were one of the actors! This was crazy—I'll never forget the feeling that I could reach out and touch things on the screen. I saw planes coming toward me and I felt that I had to escape! I still laugh when I think about it. They called this "3D," but I don't really understand what that means. You should try it!

We also went to the Boeing Museum, a place where Americans keep their memories of the wars they've fought and the airplanes they used. Americans have been in many really big wars, and each airplane on display was accompanied by information about the war in which it was used. Some were from a long time ago in Germany, and some were more recent, like the war in Vietnam. Terrible things happened in these wars.

Of course, Tanzania also had a bad time with the German government when they attacked our country and took over land in East Africa in the early 1800s, but I do not think this was the same as the wars the Americans fought. We both defeated the Germans from those past times, and this is a good thing for each country. Wars are bad, but if you have to fight one for freedom, then it has to be done. I am happy that America is a free country today, just as Tanzania is.

In this museum, there's an airplane once used by the president, and you can go on it yourself! It was fantastic to tour this plane and see the official stateroom and the dashboard in the front. It used to be in the service of President John F. Kennedy. I had heard of this man before—he is very famous.

This is in the presidential airplane for John Kennedy.

The museum contains the factory Boeing used to make its first airplanes. To me, the old planes looked like cars with wings. They also have the fastest passenger airplane ever built, the Concorde, which was surprisingly small inside. It was made in France. When I flew from Nairobi to London and then San Francisco, I was on Virgin Atlantic, and we flew in a Boeing 747. These planes were made right here in Washington State. It was very large, and all of these planes, large and small, were a new experience for me.

I have seen the moon and the stars on clear nights in the sky above Kilimanjaro. At this museum, I actually saw some rocks that came back from the moon! Can you believe this? They were on display, along with the spaceship that the Americans used to get to the moon. When the astronauts came back from that historic journey, they put this spaceship in the museum. It is scorched

Here is the picture for space at the museum. This was funny!

on the bottom from being in space. I did not know that it is so hot in space on the way back to earth, but in a film we watched, we learned about why re-entering the atmosphere produces so much heat.

At the museum, there is also a place where you can stand behind a picture and put your face through from the back. I had one taken and it looks like I'm in space and wearing a spacesuit! It is very funny. Can you imagine what people back in Tanzania said when I showed it to them? I had to tell them that I didn't actually go into space, and that this is only a photograph. No one does this type of thing in Tanzania.

To see an example of government in the U.S., my friends took me to the Washington state capitol in Olympia, where they have their parliament—though here it's called the state legislature.

Legislative governing happens inside a huge, beautiful stone building with a very large dome.

My friend Christopher served in the legislature for 20 years, and he has keys to go everywhere. They let me sit in his official seat and took my picture in it. People asked me so many questions about this photo when I got home. Everyone wanted to know if this was the White House, because it looks so important. Christopher also took my picture as I stood beside life-size statues of George Washington and Martin Luther King, Jr. These were made out of a dark metal and were very big. I am proud of my pictures, and I feel like I know more about the government in America, because I've seen it up close.

After touring the capitol, we went to a Japanese restaurant and used sticks to eat our food. I know the Chinese usually eat like this, and I've seen it done in Tanzania, but it is very difficult when you try to do it yourself! I didn't know Americans eat this way sometimes, because they don't do it when they come to Tanzania. In any event, the food was delicious—shrimp, chicken, and beef—and they cook it right in front of you on the table. It was funny to watch them cook so fast, and they made a lot of jokes while they did it.

In Seattle there's a place where you can walk onto a huge boat. You can even drive your car on the boat if you want to. We got on it and then went for a ride to another big city called Bremerton. They build many Navy ships there—again, for wars. A lot of them were parked at docks when we came into the city. I learned that you can even land war planes on these ships—those are called aircraft carriers. That seems like a good idea to me. I do not know how Americans can think of building things like this. It is amazing.

My trip to America lasted one week and I traveled to many places in Washington State. I learned a lot about this country and the people. I saw so many things when I was there. In the

Here I am sitting at the very important desk at the Legislature
where the laws for America are made.

hometown of my friends, I saw huge creatures out in the forest
where they live. They told me these are called elk. I think they
would be very good to eat, and that you could feed many guests at
a barbecue with one.

In fact, I suggested that we shoot an elk and share the meat
with Christopher and April's neighbors. Christopher explained
that you can only shoot an elk at certain times of the year, and you
need a permit to do so. That was hard for me to understand. In
Tanzania, we would never shoot an animal inside a national park,
but if it leaves the park and comes to your village, then people can
shoot it, and everyone can have something that Ghost has given
to them to eat. But things are different in America, and this is
another difference I've learned about.

People in America are very lucky to live in such a place. They have machines right in their homes that can wash and dry your clothes and it does not take long. This is a fine idea: clean clothes are very important to people in Tanzania, but for us, more work is involved to keep them that way. Many of the machines people use in American homes make life easier. People in Africa know that America is a great place, but I could not have prepared myself for what I saw when I was there. Things in Africa will seem strange and wild to you, just as the things I saw in America did for me.

Before I left to go back home, we went to another great state: California. I will tell you that story later, and also what it's like at the place they call Disneyland. But for now, let's get back to preparations for your trip here.

CHAPTER EIGHTEEN

MEDICAL CARE ON KILIMANJARO

Porters, Guides and Cooks will sing the Kilimanjaro song for you
at the end of your climb and you should not miss this.

Just ten years ago, many guides didn't speak as much English as is common now, when the level of English is usually quite high. I began learning the language in elementary school, and over the years I've picked up more from clients. I also taught classes in school when I was younger. After high school, I went to college and became a teacher. That's why my English is pretty good.

The guides get a lot of training on how to communicate with clients and how to help if they get sick or injured. This is an important part of our role. We are trained to handle various climbing-related issues, treat wounds, and administer many other types of first aid. We know how to deal with headaches, vomiting, and other small maladies that clients tend to suffer as they climb Kilimanjaro. We do medical checkups along the way; each day we check oxygen saturation levels (a measure of the oxygen level in the bloodstream) and heart rates. This routine can be reassuring if a client is having difficulties or simply feeling weak. Knowing what "normal" is, and what others are experiencing, can really help people maintain confidence. Most problems can be treated easily and will go away with time, hydration, a snack, and rest.

We usually do check-ups every morning and evening. If we see that a person is developing a condition that needs serious treatment, or decide they shouldn't continue on the climb, we can get them additional help right away. We have a helicopter in Moshi that can be deployed to rescue people in a hurry. The National Park Service takes this responsibility very seriously, and first aid training is required for certified guides

These days, it's expensive to train guides in many of the medical aspects of climbing, but the best companies conduct training programs much more frequently than they did in the past. Clients should ask about the level of medical services and training when booking their climb. You don't want accidents or injuries to happen, and neither do responsible guides, but you also want solutions if something does occur.

Sometimes we have instructors come in from different parts of the world to teach us new things about mountain medicine. I recently attended a two-week class taught by climbing experts from Montana, a beautiful and mountainous state in the western U.S. Well over half the local guides today have gone through this high level of training, and by the time you read this book, as many as 80 percent are likely to have taken advanced classes in mountain medicine and rescue. Again, check carefully to make sure the guides you hire are well-trained in basic and emergency first aid. In the past, very few prospective climbers asked these types of questions, and even fewer went to the trouble of verifying the information they were given.

In 2019, during the off-season, American experts put on a series of classes in the Tanzanian city of Arusha, and many guides attended. The guides have to pay for this training themselves, but often the companies will reimburse them for the costs of their travel, accommodations, and enrollment. The classes are technical, demanding, and expensive, but good guides really want to be prepared for anything. That is one measure of how committed guides are to keeping you safe. We care deeply about this responsibility.

Every three years, the National Park Service requires that all guides go back to school for new training. There are many aspects to this: some physical, some mental. On the job, we want to be able to help clients understand what's happening to them on the mountain, and at times this role is almost like being a mental health counselor. We learn about the technical aspects of altitude sickness, fitness, hydration, food, nutrition, and common injuries, and we use what we've learned to assure people that things *will* get better. In the rare case where something really serious is happening, we'll know what to do.

As a senior climbing guide, I only get about three hours of sleep per night, because I have so many other things to do. Senior guides have many responsibilities and duties, and we make sure that everybody on our team is well-rested before we embark on a new trip. That's a fundamental part of the preparation for all senior guides.

Sometimes, while the clients are in camp for the night, I will go and visit guides I know, or some of them may come visit me. Some companies don't want their guides to share information with other guides or with their clients. This is a competitive business, and some guides or companies will limit the amount of time you can spend visiting with other groups or talking to other clients on the mountain.

But when I see guides I know, we talk and share anyway. We like to exchange knowledge as much as we can, especially with people we know and trust. All professional guides make safety our top priority, and communication is a part of that culture. Most companies that operate on Kilimanjaro are good, but not all of them. Things are getting better, but this is something you'll definitely want to know about, prior to booking a company for your climb. This process starts with asking smart questions. How does your prospective company encourage cooperation with other guides in the interest of client safety? What is their policy on advanced and continuing training? Do they encourage and pay for these expenses and track the qualifications of their guides, especially their senior guides? Can they verify what they're telling you?

You should also know how long your senior guide has been in this business, especially if you're considering climbing some of the more non-traditional or distant routes, like the Northern Circuit or the path down into the ash pit which is in the actual crater that sits on the top of Kilimanjaro. These are complicated and challenging trips. Guides doing these should have worked their way up to this lead role with many years or prior experience as an assistant guide. Many guides will have started as a porter long ago.

By asking such questions, you help the guides know that you care about safety and will be an informed consumer. Guide services should be more than willing to supply you with answers ahead of your trip. These days, many companies offer this kind of information right up front. The more that the clients ask, the better the system will get, and this makes you safer when you travel here.

CHAPTER NINETEEN

FOOD AND NUTRITION ON YOUR CLIMB

Here is a dining tent set up at a camp on Kilimanjaro on the Machame Route.

There are two types of places to eat on the mountain. On the Marangu Route, there's a big wooden dining hall where everyone eats together. You'll sit with your own group, and though there are many groups in the dining hall, each has its food prepared by their own cooks. It's warm inside and quite comfortable.

On other routes, you will eat in a dining tent, which is set up for the evening as you arrive in camp. Groups eat in separate tents, which some people prefer. Being in a tent may not be quite as warm as a dining hall, but both approaches have advantages and disadvantages. In the dining hall, you have a chance to meet and talk to people from other parts of the world. When you're dining in a tent, you'll only be mingling with the people from your group, so you won't have as much interaction with new faces. This is something you might want to think about when booking your trip.

Most of the porters and guides either eat in the kitchen tent or in personal tents. Sometimes the senior guides will eat with the clients as well, but the porters will never eat with you. Often, the guides choose not to eat with clients because, for example, we like different food than Westerners do. This in no way is meant as an insult to you or your culture. Guides like to eat very well—they have to in order to stay healthy and strong. We eat Tanzanian local foods that we grew up with and eat at home. For example, we love a dinnertime meal that consists of *ugali* (maize porridge), *nyama choma* (grilled meat), *mshikaki* (rice mixed with local spices), and *ndizi-nyama* (plantains with meat).

It's common for the porters to not speak much English. They do strive to be polite and they might have a cup of coffee or tea with the clients, but then they like to move along and spend some time with their friends, where they can talk in their own language and share stories. Some guides are this way as well, so they too may politely share coffee or tea before wandering off. The clients usually like to talk among themselves, sharing their stories of the day.

In the old days, everyone got the same food and services, but in our time, things have changed quite a bit. Now there are many

This is the dining hall building on the Marangu Route at Horombo Camp.

different options available, because companies are trying to be more competitive and offer better services and different types of food and experiences. Food is one of the main areas of competition. Many companies are working hard to try to offer unique services and, sometimes, unique menus. Many will advertise these services up front as part of their company's promotion.

Some companies even offer vegan or vegetarian diets to their climbers. You can also tell them about food allergies, and some will tailor food to your needs. The goal is to make sure you are safe and comfortable.

Food is vital on a demanding physical climb, and you'll find that it's prepared very well. You will likely have meat and even fish high up on the mountain. Imagine being on Kilimanjaro and eating fresh fish that tastes as good as it could in a restaurant back home! It happens, because most of the chefs and cooks are highly trained. Every year we see them devise creative new menus for Western clients.

Most basic meals will start with soup and bread, along with coffee and tea, both of which are also very popular in Tanzania. Breakfast usually features hot cereal and eggs, often with meat. You will never go hungry at any meal on the mountain, and you will be provided with as much food as you can eat. Popcorn is a very popular snack option.

On the trail, you will get a lunch each day, but you'll want to take along snacks in your daypack. You'll be burning calories at a high rate, not just from the climbing, but also from the basic physical stresses of being at altitude. It will be colder up high, significantly increasing your calorie burn. To keep your energy levels up, consider bringing unusual things like freeze-dried ice cream, which is light to carry but full of calories. And if you have some ice cream left over, the porters will love it! Other good choices include hard candies and energy bars.

CHAPTER TWENTY

ALTITUDE SICKNESS, OXYGEN, MEDICATION & ILLNESSES

The crater rim of Kilimanjaro just before sunrise.
You will be feeling the altitude here.

Altitude Sickness

There is an elevation, usually in the range of 9,000 to 12,000 feet, or 3,000 to 4,000 meters, where many people start to experience a bit of altitude sickness, but there's no fixed altitude where this happens, because it varies widely for everyone. Some people never feel it at all. Some feel it at lower altitudes. Most commonly, though, people will start to get headaches as they ascend. As they begin to acclimatize, they will adjust. You should not let it bother you much, but you do need to be prepared for it.

We tell people at the pre-climb briefing that it's possible they'll suffer mild symptoms of altitude sickness, usually including headaches. Another common feeling is nausea, as if a mild stomach flu is coming on. Some people will get hit worse than others. They'll need to take a break, drink water, and eat something. This usually does the trick. Sometimes the symptoms are more serious, and the effects can be countered by descending to a lower altitude.

As I've said, the best guards against altitude sickness—that don't involve medications—are to drink plenty of water and to walk slowly. (*Pole, pole!*) In camp, it's helpful for people to lie down and take a rest after drinking water and having a snack. If they take time to do this, they'll feel much better once they settle in for the night.

When people feel any sign of altitude sickness, they understandably worry: how will I ever get to the top? We assure them that they will be fine, that if they follow the instructions, the sickness will go away, and they will continue to acclimatize and feel stronger. How you respond mentally to altitude sickness is just as important as how you treat it physically. Don't overthink it. Listen to your guides and follow their advice, and then give these solutions some time to take effect. Once you've felt what altitude sickness is like and have recovered from it, you'll be better off next time it happens, because you'll know what to expect.

Now, as you're probably aware, much more serious problems can occur if your brain swells or fluid builds up in your lungs—problems that can both be caused by altitude. These are very serious conditions (more on them below) that need to be treated right away. We can identify problems quickly and, in some cases, we'll order a speedy mobilization and rescue, with assistance from national park personnel. Other experienced guides and climbing services will help out, if necessary, when a rescue is called for. We can also call for a helicopter to take you to lower altitudes if you can't climb down on your own. This doesn't happen often, and very rarely does it happen with careful companies, but it does occur.

Altitude sickness is the main reason people don't make it to the top of Kilimanjaro, and as I've stated before, the biggest factor in determining whether you avoid it is the acclimatization process. Your climb should not be rushed, and you should not take a shorter route to reduce your time on the mountain. Never try to climb too quickly.

By the time most people get to the high camp, at around 15,000 feet, they will have suffered from headaches and maybe noticed mild nausea. (In my experience, at least 70 percent of climbers will have experienced symptoms of some kind by the time they reach high camp.) If a person rests and drinks water and has some food, they will feel better. More serious cases might involve a small amount of vomiting, but even then, it's important for people to follow the instructions and make sure they stay hydrated. It's also important that people continue to eat even if they don't feel well, because eating will ease your discomfort and give you the strength you need to keep acclimatizing.

This will seem difficult at times. When you don't feel well, you usually don't want to eat. But eating will make you feel better. You need to accept this as fact and not argue with your guides and fellow climbers. You *must* eat, even if you eat slowly at first and don't feel like swallowing anything, just take it slow and get it done. You cannot climb without eating and maintaining your energy.

It's important to understand that no one is really immune. Guides can get altitude sickness, and even experienced guides are acclimatizing each time they go back up the mountain, because the benefits of acclimatization only last a couple of days. It's more common for a guide to get altitude sickness if they've been in Moshi for two or three months before going back up to the mountain. We expect it.

Some clients have a blood chemistry profile that appears to completely protect them from altitude sickness. They create red blood cells very quickly, which is fundamentally what happens during acclimatization. With clients who won't get sick, you notice, when you do pulse-oximeter readings on them, that they maintain very high blood oxygen levels even as they ascend, when the levels of most people are dropping. (A high reading on these devices is anything above 97 percent. Low starts at around 92 percent.)

There is no way to know ahead of time if you are one of the lucky few; this just happens for no particular reason and is not associated with fitness or training. That said, fitness and training are critical to being healthy and warding off altitude sickness, but they do not by themselves completely prevent it.

Some climbers like to use Diamox to treat altitude sickness, and they find it effective. You should talk things over with your physician prior to getting or using this medication. If you decide it's right for you, make sure you have used it prior to coming to Africa, to ensure that you don't develop any unpleasant or difficult complications from taking it.

Diamox can cause people to pee a lot for the first couple of days. This can be annoying when you're trying to sleep on the mountain. The drug can also lead to other common side effects, which include tingling in the mouth and fingers. (People say this side effect lets you know the drug is working.) Diamox also seems to make carbonated beverages taste flat and metallic. I've had a few climbers tell me that Viagra can also treat altitude sickness, but I am at a loss as to how someone might have found this out in the first place, and I worry about what other difficulties taking it might present if this drug is used while climbing. I add this information only because it is curious. I have no medical basis to support its use for this purpose.

Others have said they use Diamox when they get the symptoms of altitude sickness, but not before. I'm not a doctor, so I cannot give you medical advice, and I strongly recommend that you get proper medical counseling and do plenty of research prior to using this or any other drug on the mountain. Also make sure your guides have a complete list of any medicines you are taking or might need.

I do know that people have told me that after using Diamox for a couple of days, the urgency to pee drops quite a bit, so their sleep improves. This may be a benefit to using it briefly prior to beginning your climb, if your doctor agrees. Protecting your sleep is very important.

It's interesting to observe that when people start suffering from altitude sickness high up on the mountain, or even near the summit, they only have to descend about 500 meters to start feeling quite a bit better. This is important to know because you need to be confident that even if you're not feeling well, it will only take a short amount of descending for you to feel like yourself again. It's a good insurance policy that you can cash in quickly.

As I mentioned earlier, we have a helicopter in Moshi, and it takes about ten minutes for a pilot to get into the air and over the flanks of Kilimanjaro. Believe it or not, there are people who actually hire the helicopter to take them up onto the mountain. This is foolish, expensive, and very dangerous. Do not do it. It is the slow climbing process that keeps you safe, acclimatizing along the way. Getting taken to higher altitudes by a helicopter, without taking the time to acclimatize, is very unsafe. If you think you need to do this, then you should not be on Kilimanjaro in the first place.

There are really two summits for you to think about on Kilimanjaro, the crater rim and the true summit of Uhuru Peak. Making it to the crater rim, either at Stella or Gillman's Points, is officially considered a summit of Kilimanjaro. The walk to Uhuru Peak, the true summit at 19,341 feet, earns you a gold certificate from the Tanzanian National Parks, and the crater rim at Stella or Gillman's Points gets you a green one.

Sometimes people get to the summit of the crater rim and find that they can't go any higher because they are too tired or maybe even sick. That is fine, and for the purposes of record-keeping, we guides consider reaching the crater rim a successful climb. Both are great achievements, and the certificates are nice to take home and frame. But the most important thing is to get back down safely. If the crater rim is as high as you can get, *hakuna matata!* When you need to turn around, you should not push yourself further.

Most people realize when they are done, and know they have to go down. Once in a long while, we have to carry somebody down until they feel better. Most people feeling ill are doing well enough that they can head down on their own. When they do so, they start feeling better fairly quickly. When people are on the way up, we try to encourage them and tell them that if they eat food and drink water, they'll do fine. Sometimes they're going very slowly, and it takes longer than they thought. We try to encourage people *if* we think it's safe for them to continue climbing. No guide should ever push you to keep going when you don't feel strong enough to do it safely.

Recently, when I was in training in Arusha, one of my guide friends told me that he had a client fall while climbing up from the Crater Camp with an ice ax. The ax accidentally pierced his chest between the ribs—a very serious injury. They had to call the helicopter to rescue him. He was flown to Moshi and then evacuated to Nairobi. He survived. I mention this not because I think anything like this will happen to you, but just so you know that there are medical options available if something very serious happens.

We had another guy not long ago who had his ten-year-old son with him, and they decided to jog from Stella Point, on the crater rim, to Uhuru Peak. When they got back to Stella Point, they decided to jog up there again, but the boy was starting to show signs of pulmonary edema and was getting fluid in his lungs. They were doing all this in the foolish pursuit of a record. As I've said, some people like to do crazy things on Kilimanjaro. But this is neither the place nor the time to take unnecessary risks that will imperil you or others around you.

People seeking records on Kilimanjaro are making foolish medical gambles that imperil everyone, not just themselves, and they should not be listed in any guidebooks. I will list none of them here, as this only encourages additional bad, dangerous, disrespectful, and silly behavior in others.

Oxygen

Oxygen is available on Kilimanjaro at all times to treat injured or sick climbers, but it is for medical reasons only. It should not be used to help struggling climbers get to the summit.

A few companies offer oxygen to clients to get them to higher altitudes, but I believe this practice is unsafe and potentially very dangerous. If you are already using oxygen as a fitness booster, and then you get sick anyway, you have exhausted what would have been a critical or even lifesaving treatment, and you could end up in very big trouble. You may not be able to descend to safety on your own, and you will deteriorate quickly. You might even die.

Once you get seriously sick, time is your enemy at high altitude. If the weather is bad, you can't even rely on the helicopter to assist you. This also puts others at risk, because they'll have to spend time and energy assisting in your rescue.

You have plenty of time to get fit and ready for your climb. Proper conditioning will give you what you need to make this trip a success. If you need oxygen to climb, you should not try this adventure in the first place.

Remember that there is no substitute for taking the time to climb Kilimanjaro properly. Once you've trained properly, the main requirement is that you book the correct number of nights on the mountain to allow your body to acclimatize and be safe. This is the right way to do it. There are plenty of stories of climbers who got high up on a mountain by using oxygen, only to have their oxygen system fail, and then they died a short time later. Don't let this happen to you. Respect the mountain, your abilities, and your preparations for this challenge.

Mosquitoes

The higher you get, the less you have to worry about mosquitoes and malaria, but you still need to be cautious. The areas of greatest danger are down by the coast and near Zanzibar, a part of modern-day Tanzania. We are a costal country here in East Africa, with great beaches for tourists along the Indian Ocean. As you get up onto the mountain, that risk decreases, but it's still important that visitors treat this seriously and not risk getting malaria. There are plenty of ways to avoid it.

Once you're at 2,500 meters—roughly 8,200 feet—you are fairly safe from mosquitoes, but climate change has been making it possible for mosquitos to live at slightly higher altitudes every year. Still, by the time you reach most of the villages where you start a climb of Kilimanjaro—which sit at altitudes ranging from 6,000 to 8,000 feet—you're above the areas where malaria is a serious concern. By the time you get up to the camps above the gates and the park entrance, there is little danger.

Malaria is not an illness you want to take lightly. Study the different options from medical professionals and travel experts, including your local health department. You need to make sure that you abide by your local regulations for vaccinations, or they might not let you back into your home country. You can also schedule vaccinations and get medicines to bring with you, after getting personal medical advice during such an appointment.

This may not sound specific enough for a book, but the American CDC, an authority for such matters, suggests that travelers should each do a personal risk assessment, taking into account many elements of your trip and medical conditions. Most prevention medications these days are taken prior to beginning your trip, but they are more expensive than the older ones. They also have far fewer side effects. For many years, most people used Larium, and some people still use it today, but the side effects can be significant, including upset stomach, nausea, loss of appetite, diarrhea, fever, hair loss, depression, and mental illness. Yes, it's cheap, but how do these side effects sound for your trip? I have seen people go pretty crazy for a day or so after taking it.

There are more modern prevention medications, some of them fairly expensive, like Malarone, which costs a couple of hundred dollars for a complete course. The advantage is that there are far fewer and much less significant side effects. There is also Doxy-cycline, a fairly inexpensive and older antibiotic that some people use, but you generally start it a month prior to arriving and use it a month after you have gone back home. I am told that it does not prevent infection, but keeps you from developing malaria, which is why you keep using it after you go home.

I am not a doctor. I also do not know your medical conditions. Some guidebooks will recommend certain treatments for malaria, but this does not help you make a good personal decision. All medications have pluses and minuses, and all have side effects of different types. This is something you need to decide after talking with your local health department or medical professional. Most communities have a doctor that specializes in travel medicine. Guidebooks to Tanzania are not the place to get this medical advice. Everything depends on your own personal medical history and your body. Talk to your doctor before deciding.

Diarrhea

Dietary changes and travel to different time zones can be a big cause of diarrhea. So can jet lag. Over-the-counter medications, like something as simple as Pepto-Bismol or Imodium, are often all you need, and using something that has worked for you in the past will probably be the best bet when you travel here. And the food you choose to eat can be a big help, like eating bananas, rice, or toast. Avoiding caffeine and alcohol can also be part of your short-term cure while traveling.

If you happen to come down with something more serious, like a parasite from improperly cooked food, it will be tougher to deal with. Usually this happens when people who aren't from East Africa eat food that has not been properly prepared to kill off intestinal bugs. The best insurance policy is to be very careful when eating or drinking anything. Some bugs can take a very long time to clear your system, and you'll be so sick that you may not be able to attempt your climb. Your hotel, guides, and cooks will work hard to help prevent this, but ultimately, it's up to you. If you eat barbecue cooked by a local street vendor, it will not end well. In fact, you could be sick for a month. There are some powerful medicines you can take, but you will not really find adequate treatments in Tanzania for such an illness. Your doctor can prescribe some antibiotics for such a condition, like Ciprofloxacin, and they can work quickly, but only if you bring them with you, because they will not be available here.

When you're planning your trip, talk with local health officials or your doctor about which remedies you should bring. You might want to pack different options, just in case the first one doesn't work well. And bring more than you might think that you might need. Over-the-counter medications can be shared with others if the person had a doctor who said they can take them.

Never Put Necessary Medicines in Your Checked Bags

This just makes sense, so plan on it ahead of time. Flights can be cancelled, or you can get stuck somewhere, or your baggage can end up lost for a day or so, maybe much longer. Lots of things can happen. Consider taking two sets of prescription medications, one for your checked bags and one in your carry-on bag. That way, if one is lost, you have a backup. In no instance can you plan on getting medications here in Tanzania. It's not an option. The soonest you could get necessary medications from your home country would be through a private courier service like DHL, FedEx, or UPS, and this will be very expensive to do in a hurry. Also make sure that you have copies of your prescriptions packed with each medication for legal and customs reasons, in case your luggage is checked anywhere in the world.

Other Bug Bites

There are other bugs besides misquotes that can bite and harm you, especially on safari or at lower altitudes near the coast. The yellow sac spider is one of the most dangerous and is highly poisonous, causing necrosis. The tsetse fly can cause sleeping sickness, and this is quite serious. You should keep these bites from happening, and with some thought and planning, it can be done without much difficulty.

Use physical barriers to bugs whenever possible, so they can't get to you in the first place. You will have mosquito nets in your hotel. Please use them and make sure they are tight and fully closed. Do not use scented shampoo, soap, deodorants, perfumes, or other scented personal items—mosquitos are attracted to them. Always wear shoes, and preferably boots, not only outdoors, but indoors as well. Don't wear flip-flops or sandals. Wear light-colored clothes that cover your arms and legs. Use chemical sprays—I recommend 30 percent DEET or 20 percent Picaridin—on any exposed skin.

It's very important to treat your clothes, shoes, boots, and any gear you wear, with an insecticide called permethrin prior to coming here. Be careful when handling this product when it is wet, because it can be toxic. Once applied, it will kill most insects on contact, and your clothing should be safe to wear once it is dried. Carefully read and follow the instructions on the label. Heed the directions and you will significantly decrease the chance of getting harmed by an insect bite.

When you're using sunscreen, put it on first and the bug repellent on after that, about 20 to 30 minutes later. Otherwise, the repellent will get washed away and it won't protect you properly.

Severe Sunburn

You will be at very high altitudes on your climb. The sun will be intense, and you can get an extremely bad sunburn if you are not careful. You might want to consider covering up with a light long-sleeved shirt, but however you dress, all exposed skin should be treated with high SPF sunscreen. Have it with you at all times during the day and use it frequently in exposed places on Kilimanjaro, even on cloudy days.

Check to make sure you can tolerate by trying it on at home. Some people can get reactions to certain brands at higher concentrations. You do not want to find out about such a reaction once you're already here in Africa.

Definitely bring a wide-brim hat to cover your face from the sun. You will need it. Use a hat with a chin strap and keep it on in windy conditions. You do not want to be chasing your hat down the side of the mountain. Remember to re-apply sunscreen throughout the day. Bring plenty along for yourself and others in case they run out.

Blisters

Ouch! They are not fun! The best treatment is prevention. Do a *lot* of walking in the boots you plan to bring. Buy high quality boots and wear wool socks with thin silk liners.

Do not over-tighten your bootlaces. Wear gaiters to keep out dust and rocks. Make sure you know how to put the gaiters on before you start hiking.

Make sure you have hiked on stairs and on up-and-down outdoor terrain, because your feet and boots will perform very differently on inclines. Blisters often result from the "lift" inside your boots on uneven terrain.

If all else fails and you get blisters, be sure to have moleskin and adhesive bandages, along with first aid cream to treat them. These supplies are light and small, so bring plenty. Getting blisters is usually a several-day ordeal, and you do not want to run out of materials.

HAPE

HAPE stands for high-altitude pulmonary edema. It is a deadly serious condition, and your guides know how to recognize and treat it very quickly. Basically, it is a buildup of fluid in the lungs, which can happen to some people at higher altitudes if they ascend too quickly. If you are feeling congested or are starting to cough up blood or bloody tissue, you need to tell your guide right away! Never hide this condition in the hope that it will ease up on its own. As serious as it is, it can be treated by descending in altitude. If your level of HAPE is critical, you can be put inside an inflatable Gamov bag to increase the pressure on your body; this has the same effect of taking you to a lower altitude. These lifesaving tools are on the mountain at all times.

HACE

High altitude cerebral edema (HACE) is also very serious, and your guides know how to treat it. HACE happens when the brain swells at high altitude, and this occurs because your brain tissues are expanding, usually as a result of ascending too quickly. Sometimes you'll experience a headache, which often has nothing to do with HACE, but you should let your guide know anytime your brain hurts, so they can differentiate between the two of them. One is serious and the other is not.

Confusion and delirium are signs of HACE. If you're mixing up your words—talking in what people call a word salad—then you could be in trouble. Individuals may not know they are doing this, so you should watch for it in others and tell the guides if you see it happening. The treatment often is as simple as descending in altitude. If it persists or gets worse, then a medical evacuation might be necessary. The goal is to identify it quickly and treat it right away. Just let your guide know what you're feeling, and they will do their best to keep you safe. In a properly run climb, HACE episodes should be very rare.

Other Illnesses

In addition to getting vaccinations for things like typhoid and yellow fever, you should bring other medicines you may need, like antibiotics or pain medications. Some illnesses can be treated with over-the-counter medications; others require prescription drugs. Think of the medications you typically use at home, then ask a doctor for advice on what else to take. As I have warned, you will *not* be able to buy these things in Tanzania! Proper planning is necessary ahead of time.

Consider your allergies or any other pre-existing conditions. Get the recommended information for traveling to Tanzania and East Africa from home government agencies in your home countries, and then move on from there to local medical advice.

Try to think of anything you might get at home, from indigestion to a sprain, and think of how you would treat it. Then make a plan to treat anything you might possibly encounter and bring the necessary items on your trip. Razor blades, rubbing alcohol wipes, bandages, needles for a splinter, tweezers, a small mirror and anything else that you can think of. Prepare for things you may or may not have personally experienced in the past yourself, like hemorrhoids. (Sometimes people can get them when traveling if they are not properly hydrated and strain too much when going to the bathroom.) Plan ahead and you will not be disappointed or have to ask others for over-the-counter medications or treatments. Plus, if you are prepared and have everything you might need, then nothing will probably even happen to you in the first place! Isn't that the way it goes?

Virtual Medical Care

There are excellent insurance policies available for travelers and trekkers. These can even be written for specific locations like Kilimanjaro, and they are not all that expensive. I strongly recommend that you purchase one in the event of a major illnesses or injuries. They can pay for a private jet to take you to Europe for emergency medical care. They can pay for a helicopter to fly you from Kilimanjaro to the airport. You should not need this, but if you do, it will be in place and you will get tens, if not hundreds of thousands of dollars of care without paying for it. It is a smart thing to do.

An additional benefit from many of these policies: some will provide for on-call, around-the-clock phone consultations with a medical provider if you get sick, bitten or injured. This can be very helpful to you, provide safety and peace of mind. Always check to see what options are available with different companies, and, as always, get references prior to buying a policy.

As an example, one of my clients got a tooth abscess one night before going back home. They traveled to Nairobi the next day by regional jet service and spent the night in a hotel there. The next morning, they went to a local dentist who was trained in England. The abscess had become very serious by this point and was quite painful. The insurance company found an oral surgeon on the phone, and the abscess was successfully treated. This made for a pain-free trip back to England and America.

When this client got back to America, they submitted the bill to the insurance company, which they had paid in Kenyan Shillings back in Nairobi. The company wrote a check fully reimbursing them in U.S. dollars. The company is called ihi Bupa, and they have offices around the world, with headquarters in Denmark and the U.K. If this client had been more seriously injured or had something like a heart attack or stroke, ihi Bupa would have paid the entire cost of getting them to a good facility, at little or no cost.

Medical Care in Tanzania

Simply put, you can't rely on medical care in Tanzania. If you need serious medical attention, the closest place to get it is probably Nairobi, or somewhere in Europe. Both are quite a long distance away, so come with a plan to treat most things here on your own, and an insurance policy that will kick in if you need an evacuation. Get a policy that is pre-paid for the most serious matters, regardless of how unlikely an emergency like this might be. Failing to do so can be very expensive. Virtually any serious medical procedure for a visitor will require a flight or evacuation out of country.

CHAPTER TWENTY-ONE

PORTERS, COOKS, AND YOUR CLIMB

Visiting with porters near the end of the climb at
Mweka Camp on the exit from Kilimanjaro.

Sometimes there will be as many as 20 companies, with ten clients each, at a single camp on Kilimanjaro. At other times there may be only five or ten tour operators with a single client each. You never know. The Park Service will only issue a permit for a maximum of ten clients in a single group. If you have 20 people who want to climb at the same time, they will issue two separate permits and require the party to divide into two groups. One company can take all 20 clients, but they have to be divided.

Generally, the Park Service requires four guides for every ten clients, in addition to two porters per client, along with cooks—so this becomes a pretty large group. If there are ten clients, there will be almost 40 people in that group. There will always be one chief guide and three assistant guides, which means that one of the guides will always be the senior guide in charge of everyone else, and they will make the primary decisions for that group. The chief guide is responsible for all the porters and cooks, as well as everything that happens in the group. That's a lot of responsibility.

When it comes time to select porters, some companies maintain their own list of capable people and use them over and over. They put their names in a computer and then send a message saying that a porter will be called to work on a certain day and be expected to show up. Porters have to be reliable and they need to respond when they're contacted.

The companies that use these systems contact their guides and cooks in the same way. Other companies use an older system, in which they have the guides hire porters when they get to the gate at the beginning of a climb. These are very different methods, but they both work, no matter how it may look while you're waiting at the gate to get going, everything has a purpose and is actually quite well-organized. You will be on your way soon enough, so you don't need to worry about anything. Just relax and watch what is going on.

Sometimes when I'm the chief guide, I may show up and find there aren't enough porters at the gate. If that happens, I go down to the village to recruit, which is easy for me because I know most of the porters and have worked with many of them in the past. I know what kind of a job they're going to do. A delay does not mean anything is wrong or not on schedule.

Most of the porters do a very good job and they know what they're getting themselves into, but once in a while you hire a porter that performs poorly. This makes the climb very difficult for everyone else, so guides share information with each other. After word gets around, a bad porter will have a hard time getting hired again, except perhaps by an inexperienced or low-cost guide.

We expect the porters to climb fairly quickly, so they get to the next camp well in advance of the clients. They will then set up tents and make other preparations. Once the camp is ready, the porters go out and fetch water, making sure that everything in camp is ready to go. When that job is done, they can sit back, tell stories, take a nap, or do whatever they want. In the past, porters used to have to go out and cut firewood, which was a tough job. But today, wood fires on Kilimanjaro are illegal, even for cooking.

Most porters won't speak English very well, but a few might—either way, they'll be kind and respectful toward clients. Some clients like to bring magazines or postcards to give to the porters. They really love these and they will gather in groups to share them and go over each page, one at a time, so everyone can see what's there and talk about it. They do not need to read the words to enjoy doing this. If you want to share reading material, check with the guides first to see if the publication you have in mind is permitted for your group. It usually is.

It is generally fine to give gifts to the porters, but check with the guides first to make sure it's OK. Some porters will not take things without permission, because they don't want to be accused later of having something they are not authorized to have. They want to be respectful and sensitive and not do something improper.

Not many years ago, many porters were using very poor and unsafe equipment. The Park Service is trying to make sure that anyone on the mountain has good gear, and clients can help make this happen. If you're coming to Tanzania and you have extra gear at home that you no longer use, please bring it and share it with the guides, cooks, and porters. People will be very thankful for this. A lot of the equipment that Tanzanian climbing staff use was donated by travelers. Climbing gear is the most important thing, but even simpler items, like tennis shoes to wear around camp or town, are needed. Guides, cooks, and porters will also share these items with their family. If you have space in your luggage and spare climbing gear of any kind, think of bringing it to Kilimanjaro.

Your cooks will be trained and certified by the Park Service. The cooks are highly skilled individuals who will use exacting standards to make sure your food is not only tasty but safe. This goes all the way down to the level of handling cooking utensils properly. They are usually cleaned in an iodine solution as an extra precaution.

You will probably be surprised at how well you eat on most Kilimanjaro climbs. Take note of this and thank your cooks for their hard work. They will appreciate it if you call them out after a meal to thank them, or even give them a round of applause!

Feel free to share how you're feeling with your guides and the cooks. They will do their best to help see that you are getting the food and energy you need to have a successful climb. They know how many calories you require each day to stay strong, and it will help them do their jobs if you communicate. If you get altitude sickness, eating will be an important part of your quick recovery. Your cooks can help.

Everyone on the trip, from the porters to the cooks to the guides, is part of your team!

CHAPTER TWENTY-TWO

PIRATES OF THE CARIBBEAN AND SPACE MOUNTAIN

Here I am at Disneyland and the Haunted House.

Before we get into the remaining details of your Kilimanjaro adventure—with a focus on routes—I want to tell you about the trip I took after leaving Washington State: to California and Disneyland.

This part is crazy. One day we went to the airport in Seattle and then flew to California, which took about three hours. Our destination was the famous city of Los Angeles, and this was the first time I was in an airplane that landed in the daytime. I could not have imagined what I was seeing through the window. The city was so large. You could see huge buildings in the distance, and there were smaller buildings and houses everywhere. There were mountains, and I also saw the ocean when we were heading down to the airport.

On the way in, there were many cars on the roads and on the flyovers. I did not know there were so many cars anywhere in the world. When we got to our hotel, it was very large and not like the hotels in Tanzania. It's true that hotels are nice in both countries, but this one was very tall as well. We checked in, and when we went to the rooms, I could not believe it. You do not need a key to get into your room! You just hold a card up to the door and it opens the lock. It's like magic. I do not know how this can happen, but some people have made it work this way. I have never seen anything like this.

In the morning, you can make your own breakfast in a room with other people and there is no stove there, but the breakfast is very good. Everyone serves themselves. The whole area of Disneyland and the hotels around it is so large that the people can ride a bus just to get to the main entrance, but we walked, and I think that walking is better for people anyway.

We went to the gate of this famous destination for tourists, Disneyland, and bought tickets to go inside. This is a very strange place: I do not really understand it, but it is a lot of fun. It can be

This is very funny. It is the Jungle Cruise at Disneyland.
Safari is actually much different in Africa.

very scary in some places, too. In all of Tanzania, there is nothing like this. People would be very proud to come here. It is difficult to explain. I will never forget this place and I am glad that I have the photographs to show people at home. Even then, it is hard to get people to understand just what it really is. It is like many different lands and you can go on many rides.

I can tell you that I went into a cave and walked for a long time and then we rode in a small car. You could not get out, and there is a belt to hold you in or you might fall out. That would be very bad. This road is very rough and not like the rest of the roads in America at all. There is fire there and it was very warm when we went by it. There is a huge snake! This was a big surprise. Then a huge boulder nearly hit us! I cannot say. This ride was called

Indiana Jones. We saw a movie while we were on this ride. I do not understand how people can create something like this.

We went on other rides, and one was a ride in space. We were not really in space, but this ride seemed like how it might be there. We started out seated with other people, in the light, but soon it was dark, and we went very fast. You cannot believe how fast this ride went, and the corners were very sharp. I do not know how we did not fall out, but we got back safe. I do not want to go on this again. You should be careful if you do it. They call it Space Mountain, but it is actually inside a building that is very large and round. Outside the building there is another mountain, and it looks like it has snow and glaciers on top, but I went on it is and this was not real snow or ice. On the ride, you see a creature with glowing eyes inside ice caves. This ride on the mountain is very bumpy, but it was fun. It was called the Matterhorn. They had funny music.

We went on a ride with dead people and I think this was to scare us. It is in a very old building that is in poor condition. You go into a room and it goes down, like a huge elevator, and it is dark. There is a dead guy at the top and lightning at the end. People scream and this can startle you. I cannot say what this is all about, but it was interesting. This is called the Haunted Mansion.

One very good ride happens in a boat on the water. You start in a town where people are eating. You can hear the animals and see the night sky, even in daytime! It is very dark here, just like nighttime. The boat goes on a journey and you can see many things. You will go down a waterfall, then you will hear singing. This part is fun. It is cool down there on the ride in the boat. Up on top, it is warm in California, just like Tanzania, but down in this part it is chilly. You will see treasure and other things with people who are skeletons, like they are dead.

I heard them say, "Dead men tell no tales." I do not know why they say this, but I think it is from a movie we have seen in

This Pirate place at Disneyland was very interesting,
but the pirates are bad guys.

Tanzania on TV. Then you go out into the ocean, and there is a huge ship that is fighting a war with some other people on land. I know this is not real, and that it is only for people to see, but it looks very real when you are there. There are guns and they are hitting the water with explosions. I do not think you can get hurt, but it can surprise you a lot. Then the bad people start attacking the town. You should see this for yourself. In the end, they burn the place, and you must leave. Your boat goes back up to the sun and then you get out. You are safe again. This ride was really something to see. It was called Pirates in the Caribbean.

Most of the rides are fun, even the scary ones, and we saw so many things at Disneyland. There is even an African jungle cruise, but the animals are not real, like they are in the zoo. This ride is funny. It is not really all that much like safari or Africa, but it is fun anyway. My friends told some other people on this ride that I was from Tanzania, in Africa, but I do not think the people believed this about me. I laughed a lot on this ride in the boat.

At Disneyland, there are many stores that sell all kinds of things, and several big hotels. I still do not know how someone thought of building a place like this. We had food and ice cream. The food was not all that great, but the ice cream was good. We do not normally eat so much sugar in Tanzania. We also eat smaller portions than people do in America.

I can say that this was something I could never have imagined in my life. I am glad my friends took me here before we went back to San Francisco and I got on my flight home. As I've said, my main point in telling you this story is to offer perspective. Nothing could have prepared me for Disneyland—I still can't believe it is real. Likewise, nothing can really prepare you for Tanzania and East Africa.

I think that this is a shared part of what all great adventures really are. If you have fears and are concerned about your trip and climb to the summit of Kilimanjaro, I can tell you it will be OK, just like my friends told me that the scary parts of Disneyland would be OK. You just need to trust the people who will take care of you, like my friends did for me, and like I will do if I am your guide on Kilimanjaro. You will have a great adventure, and you will get back to your home alive and safe. You will also return with stories and pictures that your friends and family will have a hard time believing, but that is also a part of all great adventures in the end.

CHAPTER TWENTY-THREE

WATER AND ACCOMMODATIONS ON KILIMANJARO

Water

One of the most important aspects of your trip will be to stay hydrated with safe drinking water. Little else is as important, and a great deal of attention should be paid to doing this properly. If you do it wrong, you can be very sick for an entire month. And I mean *really* sick, in a way that you will not forget for a long time.

The good news is that you can safely accomplish this by following simple rules, remembering that water precautions apply anytime you put water in your system in any way. This includes brushing your teeth, taking a shower, or having a coke or a drink in a hotel or bar. An ice cube in your drink can be a problem if the water was not treated properly. Inattention can lead to a disastrous result. It is easily avoidable.

You must drink only treated water at all times. On the mountain, we treat it in two different ways: by adding iodine tablets and by boiling. It's extremely important to make sure the water is safe for clients and the cooks who feed them. When we give water to

Remember that water has to be carried to many camps
on Kilimanjaro and it is heavy!

clients, it's already been treated at least once, usually twice, but many clients choose to treat it again. This is not a bad idea, and it's very important that you do not contaminate your water containers with untreated water. Please do not forget this very important step! You'll want to be careful about keeping everything clean, including the threads on top of your water container. Think about anything that can possibly touch the water you plan to drink. You need to think this over and have a plan.

I suggest that clients always treat water a second time after they obtain it from the guides. Guides are careful, but extra care is a good idea. You can use iodine tablets (which kill most, but not all, common pathogens found in natural sources of freshwater), a SteriPen (a small purifier that uses U.V. light), or one of many systems that uses a pump and filter. It's a good idea to have backups: pump systems can break, SteriPens can lose their battery charge, and you might spill or drop your iodine pills. It's not a big deal to bring multiple systems, because they are small and lightweight.

At some places on Kilimanjaro, the water can be murky, causing problems with the purification process. Filter systems can plug up, and U.V. light may have trouble penetrating the murk, so iodine tablets are your best choice here. Iodine does have some taste to it, but murky water treated with it will be safe to drink.

Under no circumstances should you limit your water consumption for any reason, since this can lead to very serious illness while at altitude. You will need to drink many liters each day to stay healthy. If the water does not look good, but it's been properly treated, don't worry: just close your eyes and drink it. There will be better-looking water the next day!

Some guide companies bring a large water purifier system on their trips. Not all companies do this, so you should ask the company you work with for specific details about how they handle water. Very few things will be as important.

We like to see each client drink ten liters of water per day if they can. This may seem like a lot, but it's a good target: the more water you drink, the healthier you will be. This amount includes the water used for your food. For direct consumption, we want clients to drink at least four to five liters per day. Anything less will make it more difficult to stay healthy and avoid altitude sickness. Staying hydrated is one of the best insurance policies you have!

A person's oxygen saturation level will get lower when they're not properly hydrated. It's important for clients to stay on top of this; don't wait for us to notice that your level is dropping. Measure it yourself with a small and inexpensive fingertip device that you can buy at most drug stores back home. These are battery operated and have a digital readout.

Another indicator: if urine is yellow and cloudy, you're not drinking enough water. This is a simple thing to monitor on your own.

Staying on Kilimanjaro

As we've discussed, there are two types of lodging on the mountain: tents and huts. They are separate systems and are used on different routes. This is important to know because they are very different experiences. Both are fine, and they are really just a matter of client choice. Some people really like the huts, which are used on the Marangu Route, which some people call the Coca-Cola Route. The name comes from this originally being considered the cheap, shorter route to the summit. I do not like this term and I don't think people should use it.

Each night, you will come to camp and get assigned to a four-bunk, A-frame hut. They are small but very comfortable. If you have four people in your group, you will get a hut to yourselves. If you are alone or have two or three in your group, you will likely share a hut with others. The beds are first come, first served, but all work fine. When you get to your hut, you will find an unoccupied bunk; put your pack and personal items there. Your duffel bag will be delivered, along with a basin of water and soap to clean up with at your leisure. Later you'll be called to dinner at the dining hall attached to your camp. In the meantime, you can take a break and rest or wander around. Don't leave your soap out in front of your cabin: ravens will take it away.

On other routes, you'll stay in tents set up by porters prior to your arrival. These are usually placed together by group, regardless of the group's size. There will also be a dining tent set up, which will be reserved for you and your group. Tents are more rustic than huts at mealtime.

When it comes time to sleep, you'll find that many of the tents are pretty large, so you'll have more room than you would in a hut. You'll be sleeping on the ground, and only the walls of your tent will be there to keep the wind out. This can be noisy. At some camps, you'll probably need earplugs.

Take some time to think these options over. They're both very good. If you are in a camp with tents, you will have far less contact with other climbers on Kilimanjaro. Some people like this, along with the more rustic experience, but others like the idea of meeting people from around the world.

An International Destination and Meeting Place

I have seen people from virtually everywhere on Kilimanjaro. They are all interesting and have their own ways of doing things. Here are some of my observations.

Quite a few Chinese are starting to visit Africa and Kilimanjaro. I recently saw a report that said 300 people from China came to go on safari in a single group. This is becoming more and more common. Chinese sometimes bring their own cooking devices and all their own food. They eat a lot of beef, potatoes, and rice. They usually have one person who can speak English and Swahili for the group.

I've noticed that Chinese clients often have not followed a good workout regimen before coming here. They basically take time off from work, get on a plane, land in Kilimanjaro, and begin their climb, and they sometimes struggle. I don't think they have a good guidebook to use when preparing for their trip. Maybe this one will help!

Some people from the Middle East have come to climb Kilimanjaro, but very few. The United Arab Emirates is one country we see represented, and we also get a number of Israelis and Turks. We get a few people from Brazil and Argentina, but not many.

Given the longstanding interest in Kilimanjaro in the U.K. and the U.S., it's no surprise that the majority of climbers come from those countries. About 40 percent of all climbers come from the U.S., between 30 and 40 percent from the U.K., and 20 percent from everywhere else. We also get a number of people from Canada.

I don't know why, but very few climbers come from France, and the number seems to be declining in recent years. More clients come from Germany than France. And of course, even with the past history of colonialization, people from Germany are most welcome today. There is no lingering resentment from what a government or people did a long time ago, and Germany was far from the only country in the world that had such policies during those times. German climbers tend to be some of the strongest and best-prepared, and they are accustomed to cold weather. They are very successful on Kilimanjaro and we like them as clients.

Most Americans arrive fairly well-prepared to climb Kilimanjaro. They have some of the best equipment of anyone in the world and tend to bring very light gear that's practical and functional. We like it when people bring good gear, mainly because it's easier for the porters to carry. When guides, cooks, and porters get equipment donated by Americans, they're very excited.

In recent years, we've been seeing more African-Americans come to climb Kilimanjaro. Sometimes it's not easy to recognize that these people are from the U.S., and at first people think they're from Kenya or some country in West Africa. But once the person starts talking, we immediately know they're from the U.S. African-Americans are very interested in the local food, history, language, and culture.

While in Tanzania you will certainly meet many people from other places in the world. Meeting people from other countries while you are on your journey can be a lot of fun!

CHAPTER TWENTY-FOUR

A SUMMARY OF ROUTES UP KILIMANJARO

This is the saddle area between Kibo and Mawenzi.
It can be part of several different climbs.

Before getting into these next chapters, I want to mention that, even if you don't choose to do the Lemosho or Shira Routes, you should read that chapter first, because I focus there on the particulars of what summit day and the descent will be like. I won't repeat that section for all of the routes, but you will need to read it to fully understand the overall experience of climbing and getting down from Kilimanjaro.

Before we get to the actual routes up the mountain, you should understand that most of them are not separate, stand-alone trails that go up and then back down the mountain. Most of them share sections with other routes, and often you will not go back down the same way you went up. When reading about the routes, you'll notice that most of them join up with others along the way. Knowing this will make the route chapters easier to understand. You can find information on many portions of other routes that also will apply to the route you eventually choose. Therefore, you should consider reading all of them, and then see which route you might be most interested in climbing. The maps should help you understand the general layout of the routes.

If you end up climbing the Marangu Route, you will go back down the same way you went up. And on this route, you will need to make sure you allow climbers going uphill to have the right-of-way, stepping off to the side when they pass. This is the polite thing to do. If you climb the Rongai Route, which is on the northern side of the mountain, and then join up with the Marangu Route on summit day, you might also come down this way as well.

Although the Umbwe Route can also be used as a descent trail, most of the other routes will involve a descent that uses the Mweka Route. This is the main way down from Kilimanjaro. On this descent, you will spend one night on the way down at Mweka Camp. We do this because you can't safely get all the way down from the summit to the park gate in a single day. Even if this was allowed, it would be very unwise to try it. You will need that extra night on the trail to stay healthy.

KILIMANJARO NATIONAL PARK
3,450M 11,320Ft. 2nd CAVE
2,700M 8,900Ft. SIMBA CAMP
RONGAI GATE 1,950M 6400Ft
3,875M 12,715Ft 3rd CAVE
3600M 11,860Ft KIKELEIWA CAMP
2,800M 9,200Ft BIG TREE
3800M 11,600Ft SHIRA-1
3,900M 12,800Ft SHIRA-2
UHURU PEAK 5,895M 19,341Ft.
School Hut
MAWENZI TARN 4300M 1400Ft
4,700M 15,500Ft Kibo High CAMP
MAWENZI HUT
2,300M 7,500Ft. LEMOSHO GATE
LAVA TOWER
KARANGA VALLEY 4,000M 13,200Ft
BARAFU CAMP 4,600M 15,200Ft
HOROMBO HUTS 3700M 12,200Ft
MACHAME CAMP 3,000M 9,900Ft
3,050M 9,900Ft MWEKA CAMP
KILIMANJARO
BARRANCO VALLEY CAMP 3,960M 13,000Ft.
MANDARA CAMP 2,700M 8900Ft
MACHAME GATE 1,800M 5,900Ft
MWEKA GATE 1,700M 5,400Ft
MARANGU GATE 1,850M 6,140Ft
KILIMANJARO

The main difference on the routes has more to do with what you will see along the way as you get started, how many people you will encounter, and how many days you spend on the mountain. As you know, the more days you spend doing this climb, the greater your chances of success. Additionally, some routes tend to be shorter and steeper—meaning you'll always be going uphill as you approach the next camp. But on some routes, you'll be on more rolling terrain, going up and down as you move forward.

This is one of the best ways to acclimatize. Any day that has you climbing to a higher point than where you'll end up sleeping is a big boost—not only to your acclimatization, but also to how you'll feel that night. On some routes that have you gaining altitude most of the time, you'll do side hikes, either as part of a day's routine or as a separate exercise on a rest day. This works very well, and you should think of planning and booking a climb that does just that.

On some longer routes, like the Lemosho, you needn't worry about this, because the acclimatization process is boosted by the time you'll spend on the trail. The Lemosho usually involves climbs that last seven to nine days, sometimes longer. The Machame Route can be a little quicker, but it still takes seven days and six nights at a minimum. These trails give you ample time to get used to altitude, and this is the main reason the success rates are high on them: from 70 to over 90 percent, for some companies. Companies that offer cheaper climbs cut costs in part by decreasing your time on the mountain. So, for example, on the Marangu Route, you might only spend three nights on the mountain en route to the top. But the success rate for doing it that way is lower—around 25 percent, or even less—so this is not a real bargain. Few people get near the summit, and a lot of them end up sick and disappointed. Some die.

Don't get me wrong: the Marangu Route is a great climb if done properly, and it has some features that the others do not.

If you book it, be careful to make sure you spend the additional nights along the way prior to summitting. In the old days, this was the main route up the mountain.

Some of the newer routes were very seldom used until recently. These days, more people are deciding to train harder so they can take on these more distant and longer climbs, in part because they think they'll see fewer people on them. The popularity of these newer routes will probably increase the total numbers of visitors on them pretty soon.

There are only three actual routes to the summit itself. They are the trails that go up to Gillman's Point, Stella Point, and through Arrow Glacier Camp up from the Western Breach. It is highly unlikely that you will climb to the summit from Arrow Glacier Camp, which sits at 4,871 meters (approximately 16,000 feet). This is a shorter way to the top, but it's not a good choice because of the high risk of rock fall, which has killed many people over the years.

The other two routes—from Gillman's Point and Stella Point—will take you more safely to the summit on Uhuru Peak. They come from either Kibo High or Barafu High Camp and are accessed by the other routes that get you to these two locations. On the Rongai Route, there is a variant that lets you get to the summit crater from the northern route, but it is similar from there on to Uhuru Peak. On this route, you can either bypass or go through Kibo High Camp or use the School Hut for the high camp. They are all pretty similar, really. You will see them on the maps in this book.

We will soon move on to the actual routes; as you learn about them, remember to look at them carefully and assess how they fit in with your own desires and goals. The biggest difference is the approach they use along the lower slopes of Kilimanjaro. If you are climbing from Marangu and going to Mawenzi and back down to

Horombo Camp before going to Kibo High Camp—as opposed to coming from the western routes like Machame, Lemosho, or Shira, or from the northern routes like the Rongai—you will almost feel like you're climbing a completely different mountain.

In some ways you are. Kilimanjaro is made up of three different peaks, Shira, Kibo (or what we think of as Kilimanjaro, defined by the highest point, Uhuru Peak), and Mawenzi. They are all part of what the original mass of Kilimanjaro was; a much larger mountain than it is today. It collapsed millions of years ago and weathering away to what it is now. Each route will take you to different parts of the old peaks that make up Kilimanjaro. Your final summit will be on Kibo. If you look at any standard picture of Kilimanjaro, that image, or what you think of as Kilimanjaro, is what we call Kibo here in Tanzania, and that is where Uhuru Peak is.

You might find it difficult to take this all in at first, but as you linger here and explore, it will all come together a little bit at a time. You will feel the rhythm of this land of Kilimanjaro begin to emerge in your thoughts, as if you had somehow been here before.

Only a few hundred years ago, Kilimanjaro was still active, and people were able to see fire, ash, and lava coming down its slopes. Can you imagine what that looked like? People in a village near a jungle and a rainforest looked up every day and saw glaciers and snow. Then, on some days, they saw smoke and fire, and at night they saw the glow of molten lava coming down the slopes and erupting into the air! It's no wonder that this land has always been one of wonder and mystery.

Even the animals were affected by this great mountain. At the higher camps, you can see the huge bones of dead elephants from long ago. At the top on Uhuru Peak, there was, for many years, the frozen and mummified carcass of a leopard. I have seen this!

Why did these animals travel so far and so high to a place where there was no food or water? When did they go there and what were they thinking or seeking? No one can ever know these things for sure. We can only ponder them and begin to feel something about them, like a piece of a memory of something we once knew. These are but some of the deep puzzles of Kilimanjaro, a mountain of spirituality, secrets and endless mysteries.

When you are climbing, taking a break, or settling in for the night, you will feel all this history surround you and speak to your soul. At times, the ancient spirits of this place and their many stories will come to you. Voices will seep into the corners of your mind as they awaken your own long and distant past. They will become a part of you forever. By coming here, you will become a chapter of the never-ending story of Kilimanjaro. Listen for the drums and the singing in the villages below. You will know that you have heard them before.

CHAPTER TWENTY-FIVE

NON-TRADITIONAL ROUTES ON KILIMANJARO

Here are glaciers on Kilimanjaro. There are many of them in the ice fields once you are on top.

I will not use entire chapters to look at each of the non-traditional routes up Kilimanjaro. You are not likely to climb one of them, and if you do, you'll have to do a lot of specialized planning and preparation—the kind of thing that doesn't belong in a general guidebook—and take into account the special costs for such a trip. If you're interested in one of these routes, you will need an excellent, top-rated guide and a serious plan, worked out well ahead of time. You can't just come here and book a trip like this.

I will go over a few of these routes, briefly, so you can get a sense of whether something like this is right for you. This is not an exhaustive list, and these days you can book pretty much anything you can think of. These nontraditional climbs will likely be quite expensive, and the Park Service will have to issue you a special permit after they've reviewed your plan, with an eye toward keeping you safe.

The Western Breach route is fairly well known. This route became quite popular after the release in 2002 of an IMAX movie called *Kilimanjaro: To the Roof of Africa*, which contained a long segment on doing the Western Breach. This movie, which was directed by David Breashears, is very good, and you should watch it if you get a chance. Your climb will be different in many ways, but the feel and landscapes of Kilimanjaro are well-represented.

If you watch it, always keep in mind that you probably won't be going up the Western Breach or to the Arrow Glacier Camp. And do not be alarmed by some of the technical climbing sequences in the film. You will not be using climbing ropes, crampons, or ice axes anywhere on of the routes you are likely to climb. Breashears is a talented and insightful filmmaker, and this is an excellent work on Kilimanjaro. I was not involved with this project myself, but I understand that it was quite an undertaking.

KILIMANJARO'S 5 ZONES
UHURU PEAK
MAWENZI
ARCTIC ZONE
LAVA TOWER
19,340 Ft
16,000 Ft
10° to 40° F
ALPINE
DESERT ZONE
16000 Ft
13,000 Ft
30° to 70° F
HEATH
AND
MOORLAND ZONE
13,000 Ft
9,000 Ft
30° to 70° F
RAIN FOREST ZONE
9,000 Ft
5,000 Ft
40° to 90° F
CULTIVATION ZONE
SUNFLOWERS
5,000 Ft
SEA LEVEL
40° to 90° F
COFFEE

I have guided on the Western Breach route many times. There have been some serious rock falls and a number of bad injuries and even deaths here, so the Park Service today encourages people not to use it. They warn potential climbers that it is much riskier and more dangerous than they might think, and they are correct. The Park Service will only let you climb it if you accept that you are doing so at your own risk. The risk is significant.

To get a permit, you'll have to show that you bought insurance that would cover the cost of a helicopter evacuation. (The danger to Park Rangers and other climbing guides is high if they're asked to do a rescue on a route like this.) You'll also have to have technical climbing gear, including an ice axe, climbing rope, and crampons. Permits are issued at Marangu Gate, the main headquarters inside Kilimanjaro National Park.

It's a beautiful route, but it's tough. The climb shown in Breashears's movie took more than a month to complete, and even though the movie is a great story, it is not an accurate, practical description of the climb you will be making. In any event, you should only consider doing this if you are a very proficient climber with technical equipment.

I have done every route on Kilimanjaro. I've also guided many expeditions doing research on the mountain, sometimes on trips that did not involve any of the regular routes. One time, while guiding a group of scientists who were studying glaciers and climate change by setting up weather stations on icefields, I got lost in a heavy snowstorm.

This was challenging: there were no routes in this area and the terrain was extreme. When we started out that morning, conditions were great, but a storm blew in and things changed rapidly. It was freezing and the winds were very strong—so strong at one point that we had to sit down because we could no longer walk without falling. It took us almost seven hours to get back to a main trail.

You have to keep your head in conditions like this, and your guide must be a good and confident leader. When you're not on a route that is well-established and marked, situations can become very dangerous in a hurry. You need to know exactly what you're doing and have the background to deal with emergencies. I mention this because, if you're thinking of booking a non-traditional route, it is imperative that you only book with the most experienced guiding services. And, obviously, keep this in mind in case you're thinking of going off the trails on your own.

During other climbs I've guided for scientists, I've also been to the huge ash pit that sits at the bottom of the large crater on top of Kilimanjaro. This is a great sight and almost otherworldly. It takes about three hours to descend from the summit of Kilimanjaro to the ash pit. It's a fairly long walk—roughly several hours long, and this is only one way! You can get to the ash pit from Stella Point, or you can come up via the Western Breach Route. It is a very tough climb back out, all uphill until you return to the crater rim. Few regular clients want to go to the ash pit or the volcanic crater, but it's a trip I'll do if people want to try and if they seem fit enough to handle it.

Some people *think* they would like to go to the ash pit, but they find that they're too tired or are not feeling well enough once they get to the summit. It takes about six or seven more hours of climbing to go down and back, and most people cannot do it. I would ask you to really think it over if you are contemplating it. You will be paying for it up front, no matter if you get there or not.

And remember—this is very important—you will be climbing *down* to the crater and ash pit, and then, after the most difficult day of your life, you will have to climb back *up* to the crater rim to return to Mweka Camp for the night. There is no other option besides returning to camp. You can't just give up and stay at the top safely overnight. There is no tent or camp, and it will become extremely cold and windy once the sun goes down. It is rewarding but far more difficult than you might imagine.

One less conventional route that I will cover in detail is the Northern Circuit Route. It is not commonly used, but it is becoming more popular, so I will go over it later. It is a viable route for very well-prepared climbers who understand and accept the risks.

CHAPTER TWENTY-SIX

THE UMBWE ROUTE

The Arrow Glacier and Camp from the summit of Uhuru Peak.

Very few climbers do the Umbwe Route, somewhere in the range of five percent or less. It's short and steep—the incline on this climb is roughly 53 percent—and it doesn't offer enough time or distance to acclimatize properly. For some people, a very small number who are very physically fit, it's a good route. I don't care for it myself, and that's why I didn't put an itinerary for this route at the start of this chapter.

You may be getting the idea that I am trying to discourage you from climbing the route. You are completely correct! I know it well and do not think that it is a good idea except for a very few people. Even they will likely get sick when doing it.

There are, however, some benefits to this route. You won't see many other people, and I have to admit that some of the most remarkable views of Kilimanjaro are found on the Umbwe, thanks to the sharply vertical terrain. That said, I do not plan to return to the Umbwe Route anytime soon, so if I guide you, our path to the summit will involve a different trail.

But if you just can't keep yourself from trying this, because the challenge feels right for you, here are a few things you'll need to know.

You're first stop will be the Marangu Gate, to get your permit. Then you will proceed to the Umbwe Gate, which is the start of a long and rough jeep trail that requires four-wheel drive.

As you begin the climb, you will enter a dense, beautiful jungle that is rough and steep. The start of this route is the hardest part, and it will be hard to catch your breath for a long time. This jungle area is very wild, and the absence of other climbers will make it seem wilder. This part will take roughly six or seven hours to do, assuming you can keep up a reasonable pace.

On this portion of the climb, you'll will gain more 1,000 meters (roughly 3,000 feet) in a very short distance. There are always good water sources at this location, and you will find a cave at the top at 2,940 meters. This is a good place to camp for the night.

In the morning, you'll head out, still in deep jungle, and after about an hour you'll suddenly break into the open and be rewarded

This is the climb to Barafu Camp on Kilimanjaro.

with an almost indescribable view of the summit of Kilimanjaro and the Breach Wall. It is hard to explain how amazing this view really is. Staying an extra day to take it all in is a good idea: you'll get more time to acclimatize and to contemplate this amazing sight. There is no camp or water here, so come prepared. Like all other routes of on Kilimanjaro, you must come here with a proper contingent of guides, porters, and cooks for your group. They will have to haul water and set up your camp.

As you continue along this path, it will get steeper in the moorland zone—one of the entirely separate climate zones on Kilimanjaro that you will pass through—and after a while the route levels out some. You'll wander along until you come to the Barranco Camp at 3,960 meters (13,000 feet), one of the most beautiful locations on Kilimanjaro. This spot is somewhere around five or six hours from the Umbwe Cave Camp.

The steepest part of the Great Barranco Wall. It is not that difficult.

This area has already passed the Lava Tower and you will need to go back a couple of hours to climb the Western Breach Route, which in the previous chapter, I have already suggested that you do not do in the first place. The Umbwe Route is commonly used to get to the summit via that dangerous route, one that the park service now recommends that climbers do not use. The other option, the more sensible one, is to continue up the Machame Route to the Karanga Valley and then to the high camp at Barafu the next evening. Your summit bid would begin the next morning. In the past, some people doing the Umbwe Route have skipped the Karanga Valley Camp, because they were in a hurry.

Think about this. The trek involves one night at Umbwe Cave, one at Barranco Camp, and one at Barafu High Camp. Even with a stay at the Karanga Valley, that's only four nights, far too little time to climb all the way from Moshi to 19,341 feet! Unless you are in remarkable shape, you probably won't make it, and you could become seriously ill from altitude sickness even if you are in perfect condition.

Could you do this route by spending a few extra days at camps along the way? Yes, and you could also climb above the camp each day and go back down for the night to acclimatize. (Remember the climb-high/sleep-low concept? It will help a lot here.) With that type of planning, this is a viable, though a very steep, route. But don't do it if you're just hoping to save time and money. Do not underestimate how difficult this grade is when climbing. Very few people will like it.

Do not be discouraged: I wanted to get this route out of the way first, and there are other paths that are far easier. On these routes, you will encounter few difficulties that can't be handled by any properly prepared climber.

CHAPTER TWENTY-SEVEN

THE LEMOSHO AND SHIRA ROUTES

The deep jungle areas on the lower slopes of Kilimanjaro are amazing.

Route Summary

Days: 8 – 9 (7 to 8 nights, but it can be done in 6 nights/7 days safely by skipping Shira 2, however the extra night is a good insurance policy for the summit!)

Length: Usually about 45 miles or 73 kilometers, depending on the exact route

Elevation Gain: Roughly 3,200 meters or 14,000 feet total, but depends on the exact route

Starting Point: Londrossi Gate 2,300 meters or 7,500 feet

Camps (nights) along the way:

Big Tree	2,800 meters or 9,200 feet
Shira One	3,800 meters or 11,600 feet
Shira Two (optional)	3,900 meters or 12,800 feet
Barranco Valley	3,960 meters or 13,000 feet
Karanga Valley	4,000 meters or 13,200 feet
Barafu High Camp	4,600 meters or 15,200 feet
Mweka Camp	3,050 meters or 9,900 feet

The Lemosho Route is one of the very best for acclimatization because of the amount of time you'll have on the mountain: you can do it in anywhere from seven to nine days. I really like this climb, which has become much more popular in recent years as people have come to understand that longer climbs are better. More and more people are beginning to take advantage of this concept.

It takes about two hours to drive from Moshi to the start of the route. In 2017 or so, Tanzanian National Parks made improvements to the road leading from Moshi to the starting point at Londrossi Gate. Thanks to these major changes, about half the road is now really nice—not up to what you may be thinking of back home, but really good by Tanzanian standards—while the rest is still a bit rough, and it can be almost impassibly muddy when it rains. If your trip isn't in the rainy season—and I recommend it not be—the drive will be fine, but hold on during the rugged parts.

The drive from Moshi to Sanya Juu, a city near the southwest portion of the national park, goes through many beautiful and interesting villages and small towns. Proceeding on the improved road, you'll drive through the Boma Ng'ombe area, home to just under one million people; Sanya Juu, is home to 600,000.

Most who live in these villages are farmers. All these areas are on the slopes of Shira, one of the three volcanic peaks of Kilimanjaro, and the land is very fertile because of the volcanic soil. There are pine trees in this area, sometimes used for furniture and other products, and the farmers grow many vegetables, including maize, yams, and cabbages. They used to grow more coffee and cotton, but because of climate change, they are now switching to crops that are more drought-resistant, like sunflowers and casava. The rains, although heavy, are becoming less predictable in recent years. The people who live in the villages are very friendly; they would welcome you warmly as a guest.

We will normally check you in at Londrossi Gate, where all the climbers doing this route sign in. The porters will weigh all the equipment and packs they'll be carrying. Then we load everything back onto the top of the Range Rover-type vehicles and drive clients and supplies to the starting point. It can be pretty crowded at the sign-in, and this process takes time. Park officials are working on changing this, to allow people to sign in at the Lemosho Gate itself. They hope to have the facilities there updated and this change underway sometime in 2021.

It takes about one or two hours to get people signed in and then ferried back over to the starting point. You will just need to relax until the group you're in gets permission to start climbing. The timing depends on how many clients you have and how many other groups are waiting to sign in. The Park Service spaces the departure times of the different groups, so they are not all starting out all at once.

LEMOSHO MACHAME ROUTES
UHURU PEAK 5895M. 19,341 Ft.
STELLA POINT 5,756M. 18,652 Ft.
MWENZI
BARAFU CAMP 4,600M. 15,200 Ft.
KARANGA VALLEY 4,000M 13,200,00 Ft
BARRANCO VALLEY
BARRANCO CAMP 3,960M 13,000 Ft.
SHIRA-1 3,800M 11,600 Ft.
BIG TREE 2,800M 9,200 Ft.
LAVA TOWER
EXIT PATH ONLY
LEMOSHO GATE
KILIMANJARO
2,300M 7,500 Ft.
SHIRA 2 3,900M 12,800 Ft
MWEKA CAMP 3,050M / 9,900 Ft
MACHAME CAMP
RELAX 3000M 9,900 Ft
MACHAME GATE 1,800M 5,900 Ft.
KILIMANJARO
KILIMANJARO
MWEKA GATE 1,700M 5,400 Ft.

The upper slopes of this route are very open and rocky.

There is a shelter at Londrossi Gate that is similar to the facilities at the Machame Gate. The Park Service is planning to build a nice facility with a good washroom and a place for people to stay. Having these types of facilities is really nice when you're signing in, but don't be fooled: the nice restrooms at the gate will not be like the ones that you will use higher up on the mountain!

There's no store at Londrossi—like the one that exists at the Marangu Gate, where you can purchase foods, items, and books. In fact, there's nothing like that on the entire northwestern or northern side of the mountain. The Mweka Route has many facilities and places that serve visitors, because that's where, these days, almost everyone ends up after they descend. You won't find such facilities here: there is no Blue Zebra or showers or a restaurant.

I would expect that many locations like this will be developed in the future, thanks to increased demand and the desire to create opportunities for vendors.

Not too long ago, a route like this was very unpopulated—that's what originally drew people to it. Other people were also beginning to look more closely at climbing statistics and success rates, and it was easy to see that a longer route like this led to more success. Trekkers realized they had far greater chances of seeing wildlife; in the lower elevations, the route winds through a great forest where you'll see blue and colobus monkeys.

Today, the Lemosho Route is to some extent a victim of its own success. With so many people climbing it, the animals are starting to move further away from the area. That said, it's still an excellent route, one of my favorites.

Trash & Route Popularity

Route popularity changes all the time on Kilimanjaro, and it may have shifted by the time you read this book. Why this happens will take a short explanation, and then we will move on to the rest of this route.

Changing popularity of different routes happens because of a similar pattern to what occurred with the Marangu Route, which lost popularity because of the high numbers of people going there and the trash they left. We local guides and government officials were taken by surprise in the early to mid 2000s: we were not quite ready for so many people to start coming to Tanzania all of the sudden! Soon, too many people were climbing the Marangu Route in a sloppy way, leaving behind a lot of trash, and we did not have all of the policies we needed to help keep the mountain clean. Much of that has changed, and the Park Service keeps making improvements everywhere on Kilimanjaro. If you're reading an older guidebook, these changes may not be reflected yet but they're real. We are now trying to carefully educate people about their responsibilities when they come here. Cracking down on unscrupulous and illegal or unethical operators in Tanzania and abroad is part of the process.

Trash had become a problem on the Lemosho and Shira Routes as well, but we're making great strides in getting this under control. You can help by doing your part. This route is undergoing major upgrades, so please be patient, realistic, and prepared for what the conditions will be at the time of your arrival. Good guides can tell you everything you need to know about current conditions. They will keep you safe. You need to take the initiative and learn as much as you can. Stay in touch as your trip gets closer, and participate actively in making your climb a successful and fun adventure.

I would not discourage you from considering other more popular routes, like the Marangu, because of inaccurate information contained in older books. What was true at one moment in time will most likely be very different today. Do not avoid a route because it has a bad reputation that may be out of date. The park service has made many improvements and changes in recent years to keep all routes up to much higher standards.

At the same time, do not expect to see a lot of large animals, like elephants or buffaloes, on a route that only a few years ago had very few climbers on it. Most routes, except the Northern Circuit, are pretty busy these days, and animals tend to move away from them a bit.

Back to the Route

You will find that the forest is very dense near the Lemosho Gate, more so than at any of the other entrances where you start a climb. There is still a lot of wildlife in this area—though you may not see it at first. In the past, climbers were likely to see elephants and buffaloes when they began this climb. These days, most of the animals have moved along because of human crowding, so it's unlikely you'll see these larger animals right at the gate where you start.

In the thick, dense jungle at the start of the climb, you *will* see many monkeys, and they will be very close to you. In the Marangu area, monkeys are less common because they've been hunted for food. This has not happened yet at the Lemosho Route gate; this area has very few poachers, which leads to more animals living close to the trail and next to the villages.

There are two types of monkeys in this area: blue monkeys, which are on the smaller side, sort of like the size of a small dog you might have as a pet, and so-named because they have blue balls that stand out against their mostly black fur! The larger species is the colobus monkey, a black-and-white primate that can weigh 15 kilograms (32 pounds)! They live in the treetops, and they're fun to watch as they glide from limb to limb.

On this route, there's a chance you'll see a famous type of large antelope called the eland. They're usually found at the boundary of the rainforest, right when you enter a more open area, the Heath and Moorland Zones. The zone starts at about 2,700 meters (9,000 feet) and continues up to about 4,000 meters (13,000 feet). Your trek through the rainforest is about seven kilometers long on this route.

Most climbers are very excited to begin the climb and see such exotic surroundings. The hike in the dense rainforest is a whole new experience for them. I find, too, that it can be scary at first because of the thick jungle. Even though you won't see many buffaloes or elephants on this route anymore, you will see buffalo and elephant dung on the trail. Clients start to worry about running into one of these large creatures. I find that people tend to stay close to the guides during this part of the trip!

A Brief Note on Elephants

You are more likely to see elephant here than anywhere else on the mountain these days. A little more than a decade ago, there were a lot more larger animals along this route, and back then we were always accompanied by a Park Ranger with a gun, in case there was a problem with an elephant or buffalo. About 11 years ago, the Park Service stopped this procedure. Sometimes the elephant dung we see is still steaming, so people think the elephants are very close by. We tell them not to be frightened and not to worry. You would be very lucky to actually see an animal. There is no serious danger.

Besides, elephants are friendly to people. The only way an elephant would be a danger to you is if you provoked it. I have found that the older elephants are the friendliest. They move very slowly and sometimes they might come up close if they want to check you out. If you see an elephant, just listen to your guide and carefully follow their advice. There is no reason to provoke or bother an elephant. They are wild animals. If they want to approach you, let it be their choice.

Younger elephants will generally run away if they see you. I've had elephants get to within 100 meters of me on Kilimanjaro, and that's about as close as they generally get. They're happy with that distance and so am I. I have had elephants get to within 10 meters of me on Mount Meru when I was walking on foot, but they seldom do this on the Lemosho Route. Because of their great size, this can seem pretty close when you are on foot. Just keep moving slowly and take pictures as you walk by. Some elephants get very big—up to 13 feet tall and 16,000 pounds, with long tusks. If big elephants are close, you want to let them know that you're in the area and not surprise them. Your guides will know what to do. It will be very safe, and a sight you will never forget.

Back to the Route & Shira Alternative

There's an older, alternative trail called the Shira Route that takes you up to the Shira Plateau—a different starting location from the one we've been talking about. Going this way used to be more common, but people today are more interested in seeing the beautiful dense forest on the Lemosho Route. The old Shira Route is kind of like a road, and there are portions of it that you can actually drive up in a vehicle. Doing that is a bad idea for a number of reasons. Obviously, it's not very scenic compared with a jungle trail, and you should be gaining altitude slowly, not at the pace of a vehicle.

There is also the possibility of leaving the dirt road and hiking along this side of the mountain. I know this route and it is safe. It will make your trek longer and your acclimatization will improve. But you will miss the forest on the Lemosho Route, a really great part of the trip once you get used to the thick jungle.

When doing your research, either in books or online, you will find a lot of different information on this Shira Route, and it is often listed as the beginning of the Northern Circuit Route as well. It seems to have a "gate" at a number of different locations that range from 7,500 feet to 11,800 feet. The reason for this is the road. A number of companies begin their climb at this higher location by driving you there. This is a terrible idea, and you should not do it.

If you fly to Tanzania and are then taken right to 11,800 feet to begin a climb, you will get sick and not enjoy yourself. It is a big mistake. If you are told that you will start your climb at "Shira", it is imperative that you find out the altitude of your starting point for your trip. You can begin a Shira climb at a lower altitude and then slowly work your way up, but this takes most of another day, however it is the proper way to do it. An alternative is to just use the Lemosho Gate, even on the Northern Circuit Route if you wish. Using Shira as a starting point requires additional information on exactly where your climb will begin.

Continuing on the Lemosho Route

When you're going up the Lemosho Route, you will leave the rainforest on the second day and emerge into the Heath and Moorland Zones, an environment that is very different from the jungle. The deep forest will give way to much more open ground with smaller and more sparsely spaced trees and vegetation. You will camp the next night on the beginning of the Shira Plateau. The first camp is called Big Tree in English, and in Swahili is *Mti Mkubwa*. This is a very interesting place for you to see.

You will see a big wooden building on the Shira Plateau—this is the headquarters fort for the Rangers, and it's the staging area they use if a rescue becomes necessary. Climbers and guides do not use or stay in this building. As usual, the clients will all have personal tents for sleeping and a communal eating tent as well.

Earlier on the climb there are a lot of stinging nettles and sometimes many bees. This is the upper edge of this zone where they occur, from the jungle up to here. People are afraid of them as well.

You should be very careful of the stinging nettles in the lower altitudes. If you touch one of them it's not good. If you get stung by a nettle it is extremely painful and sometimes can cause a fever. It's important to listen to your guide to be careful not to get stung by a bee or stinging nettle. It can take up to 12 hours to feel better

Lava Tower is very high. You might take a side trip here to adjust to the altitude.

if you get stung. Try to identify these plants and stay away from them. Your guides will tell you what to watch out for. We call these nettle grasses. It's uncommon for people to be stung by bees. If you do not disturb the bees, they will not bother you. Just leave these African bees alone.

The second camp on the Lemosho Route, about seven kilometers from the first, is on the Shira Plateau, and it's called Shira Camp. We also call it Shira 1. There is a second Shira Camp that we call Shira 2, and this is where the Machame Route joins up with this one. You might want to have to look at a map to see where they come together. After you reach Shira 2, then the routes are the same all the way up to the summit.

When you come out of the jungle, on either route, the country really opens up and looks quite different. It happens suddenly and it surprises people as they climb to the rim of the old crater. Shira is actually the most western part of what was once the ancient mountain of Kilimanjaro, when it was much larger than it is today. Now it is one of the three summits that make up Kilimanjaro, and though it technically is a "peak," to you it will look more like a type of a crater on a high plateau.

From the edges of the crater, you can look onto the main part of this very high plateau. It's a surprising experience, because you can suddenly see so far and a large expanse opens up before you. This big, flat area was once the Shira volcanic crater.

More than 90 percent of the people who make it to the Shira Plateau will continue their climb; only a few decide that this is as far as they can go. It becomes pretty obvious to both client and guide when someone is not able to continue past this point: they just were not physically prepared. Most of the turnarounds happen at high camp, not here. But if you've made it to Shira and still feel OK, you've got a solid chance of making it to the top.

From this point forward, people have a couple of options. Some spend time at the second camp at Shira for acclimatization. Some continue on past the Lava Tower and onto the Barranco Camp. (At that point, you'll be joining up with people who took the Machame Route.) You can also take a side trip over to the Lava Tower from this route—it's a sight worth seeing and another good way to acclimatize.

Lava Tower trail, between Shira 2 and the Barranco Valley, is the center of an old lava tube that rises straight up into the air and is a distinctive feature of this part of Kilimanjaro. The trail here is also fairly close to the elevation of the high camp you'll stay in before you summit. Most good guides will want to take their clients there for acclimatization, then descend back down the trail to Barranco Camp. Clients like to go there because it's a fascinating experience in its own right. For some clients who are having a

The Barranco Valley is on the Lemosho Route.

little more of a difficult day, guides use this trip as a way to assess how they'll probably fare on summit morning. Climbing Lava Tower itself is a technical endeavor that requires serious climbing equipment. You will see people doing this in the IMAX movie, but you are unlikely to try it on your climb.

Lava Tower is a good place to measure your own performance. You should be feeling the altitude here and take note of your responses. This will help you prepare for your summit day, only a few days away now.

Leaving either of the Shira Camps and continuing along this route, you will now be going down into the Barranco Valley, which is an amazing experience. The place is almost magical because of the many types of plants and trees, some of which, like giant groundsel and lobelia, can be seen nowhere else in the world. When people get to the Barranco Camp, they'll see the Great Barranco Wall in front of them, and many climbers start to feel concerned that climbing it will be too difficult. But it looks harder and more intimidating than it really is. There is a good route to the top. The path is well- worn in the rocks, and there are good foot and hand holds along the way that are not apparent from below. Just take it slow and easy and don't worry about it the night before.

The Barranco Valley is a place where the guides like to pause and spend more time with clients, to talk with them and calm their nerves about climbing the wall. Throughout dinnertime, this is often the main topic of discussion. As we sit and look out over the valley, the clients keep asking us over and over where we'll go and where the path is. The view from this camp in the evening is amazing.

In the morning you will continue down into the valley and do a small stream crossing. When you start up the other side, you will begin in the shadows of the morning. As you go up the wall and out of the shadows, you will see Mount Meru in the distance. This is one of the most remarkable views anywhere on Kilimanjaro. Going up this route, you will also see one of the classic views of the top of Kilimanjaro. You have probably seen this view in many publications and picture books. It generally takes about two to three hours to go from Barranco Camp to the top of the wall. People go slowly, which greatly assists them. It is not a particularly difficult or dangerous section.

When people finally get to the top of the wall, they are very happy. They also say they would not want to go back down this way on the way out. We tell them that this is not the route back, that clients are finished with this part. Most of the clients thank you at this point and are very happy about their accomplishment. They're

Karanga Valley Camp.

proud of themselves, and their worst fears were not realized.

I have had a few people who said they did not want to even try this part of the climb. I've never had anyone turn around during those three hours once they started. The few people who did not want to try were simply helped back down off the mountain by a junior guide. The people who begin this day do just fine. You will as well.

If a person decides not to continue on the climb, the way down from here is the Umbwe Route. This is a very steep climb, but we try our best to make sure that the clients are always safe, no matter what decision they make. It is inconvenient to have to send a guide down with a client, but it happens. This is one reason why good climbing companies always have at least one extra assistant guide along on any climb, no matter how many clients they have.

The next day you will do an up and down, dusty trek to the Karanga Valley Camp. This is a nice day for acclimatization: you will climb down into some smaller valleys and then back up to higher elevations. This is a beautiful side of the mountain. In the valleys you will see water and interesting plants. There are curious rock overhangs on the side of small creeks at the bottom. None of the downhills or uphill sections are so long or steep that they are too difficult. It is a good day on the mountain for most people and it will not seem that long. The entire distance is only about five kilometers (three miles), and you will complete it in about four or five hours.

In the morning, as is true most mornings, there will be a dense fog in the valley below, and on most days, it will rise up to your camp. As it burns off, you'll see the mountain below you begin to open up, as the fog and clouds seem to withdraw down to the East African plains. You will also see heavy moisture that comes back in each night. This is how the plants get much of the water they need when we aren't in one of the two rainy seasons. Without this nightly wetting of the ground in these sparse upper forests, this part of Kilimanjaro would be a desert, and not the lush green garden of exotic plants you see today. The area is filled with life because of these evening mists.

You may have seen the footprints of buffalo or other animals along the way in this area, or near Lava Tower. These animals would not be there either without the nightly clouds and moisture they bring. In the morning and late in the evening, these clouds and fog will cover the lower portions of Kilimanjaro. During those times, you can look out and see Mount Meru rising far above the clouds below. It is a remarkable sight.

A Few Comments About the Night Sky

Although the summit of Kilimanjaro is a destination you want to attain, and you soon will, there are parts of the journey you should not miss along the way, and taking in the views up here is one of them. You are now at the Karanga Valley Camp. When the sun sets, Meru is surrounded by an amazing light show of orange and reds as the day comes to an end. When the sun is finally gone, the air becomes very cold, and the Southern Cross comes out to welcome you to these lands near the equator. This is a sight you've probably never seen before, and it looks quite different from this particular camp.

Some people wake during the night at this altitude or have to pee. They might leave their tent to go out and see the night sky. At higher altitudes like these, you will see stars that are almost hard to imagine. You can clearly see the Milky Way and feel like you could reach out and touch it. Of the many experiences you'll have on your trip, this is among the most wondrous. Even if you sleep well during your climb, I hope you get a chance to go out at night and see it a few times.

There is a book I'd like to recommend to you called *Hawaiiki Rising*, which is about the ancient mariners from the islands of Polynesia in the Pacific, and the voyages of a boat called the *Hoku-le'a*. In long-ago times, these mariners explored the most remote portions of the world in large canoes with sails, and they did it without iron or compasses. They sailed to new lands thousands of miles away using a navigating system called the "star compass," in which they used the positions and movements of the stars to plot an accurate course. Using this system, they were able to sail over 4,000 kilometers from Tahiti to Hawaii in about a month. Their navigation was remarkably accurate.

Westerners refused to believe that non-white and non-Christian people could have accomplished such feats of navigation, but it was true. They also perfected the use of sails and sailing vessels. By the time that Captain James Cook came to the islands of Hawaii, the Polynesians had large sailing canoes that were three times as fast as any Western ship. After Cook's return to England, the information he provided about Polynesian navigation and sailing was suppressed for generations, because of ignorance, religious intolerance, and racism.

Many ancient civilizations like these—including ours here in Africa—rivaled or exceeded those of the Europeans in science, trade, and culture. When you see this night sky, exactly as these ancient mariners did from these very same latitudes, you will be filled with wonder about the ancient travelers and cultures who came long before the modern Europeans. As we have discussed, East Africa is the land of the original explorers who went to the far reaches of the earth. The spirit of the African and Polynesians explorers kept that dream of discovery alive for generations.

A replica of the original *Hokule'a* was built not long ago and sailed between Hawaii and Tahiti, to retrace the journeys of those early explorers and prove that it could be done as their ancient legends had stated. The boat was also recently sailed from Hawaii to Africa. They did this to honor the memory of the original travelers who had come from this land. Nowhere else on earth will you see the night sky and the ancient "Star Compass" in just such a way as you will from this camp.

Back to the Route

In the morning, it will be time to move to your last camp along this route, the Barafu High Camp. This is a day when you'll feel something different happening. It's not a long distance to Barafu High Camp, only about five kilometers (three miles), but you'll begin to sense that the final push is not far away. The trail will climb from here. It's not a steep or demanding journey, but you're starting to get into high altitudes, reaching 4,600 meters (15,239 feet) at Barafu. It will take you about five hours to get there, at a very slow and leisurely pace. Now is not the time to push yourself harder. You will need all your strength tomorrow for the last push to Uhuru Peak. Do not forget: *pole, pole.* Take it easy along this path. You will get there soon enough.

The land up here is barren and cold, dotted all around with large boulders. At night the winds will rise up, and your ear plugs might come in handy at bedtime. It might even be windy inside your dining tent. This can trouble people, but you should try not to worry about it. Your guides have been here many times, and everything will be fine.

Try to eat no matter how you feel, and drink plenty of water. You and your fellow climbers will feel excitement and anticipation. You will have many questions and your guides will answer them. In truth, the summit is not all that far away by this point— only about seven kilometers (four miles)— but the next morning will be a big challenge, for a number of reasons. Some of them are real; some are only imagined. You remember earlier when we talked about mental preparation? Yes? Now it comes into play.

At this point in the climb, some people will be overcome with fears that are far more imagined than real. This is OK; the experience is new to you, and uncertainty is a natural reaction. Others will be excited and want to get started on the final portion of the climb. In either case, it's important to visualize success. Don't spend time looking up at the mountain and thinking about how far you have to go. Focus on going one step at a time and visualize yourself standing on top and then heading back down. See yourself filled with joy and accomplishment! Your certificate and a beer will be waiting for you and your fellow climbers down at your hotel! You can do this!

If you end up feeling too sick or weak to continue, then by all means don't. But be sure that it's not just your nerves and the wind that are troubling you. The sun will rise again, and the wind will die down. That evening, eat as much dinner as you can and load your final pack for the morning. Check your laminated list for the items you'll need for the last push to the summit. This is very important: do not pack in the morning. Do it before you go to bed and do not trust your memory at these altitudes. Use your checklist, and double-check it.

This will not be just another normal night on the trail. You will eat, pack, and go to bed very early, and you probably won't get much sleep. In most cases, you'll be getting up before midnight for what will be a very long day. Don't leave water in your bottles without insulated covers on, or your water will most definitely freeze and become unusable. This would be a serious mistake. Take care if you need to go outside at night to pee. It can take a long time to warm up again when you return to your tent and sleeping bag. The winds can be strong and cold.

Don't spend time playing cards, listening to your iPod, watching the night sky, or visiting at this location. It's time to go to bed and get as much rest as possible. Use your ear plugs to block out the wind. Don't worry if you find it difficult to sleep; even lying still and just resting is good for you. You will sometimes be in a state where you can no longer tell the difference between being asleep and being awake—they begin to merge together. This is OK. It all counts as rest and you need as much as you can get.

Usually at around 11 to 11:30 PM, someone will come to your tent to wake you for breakfast and a final summit day briefing. This is the point when some people seriously think of calling it quits, but most will continue on. Eat and drink as much as you can. You will soon be on your way in the darkness, and you'll already see the lights of other climbers snaking up the trail ahead of you. If there happens to be a full moon, you'll see a surreal light in the night sky showing the way. Many people specifically book their trips during the time of a full moon for this reason. The moon is so bright that it will actually hurt your eyes to look directly at it!

It will be very cold at first, but it won't be all that long before you begin to see the sun rising over the East Africa plains. This starts around 4 A.M. The light will warm your soul and you will feel its energy embolden you. The first hours in darkness will be slow, and you will be breathing hard with every step you make. The ground will be soft with small pumice rocks, and it is sometimes discouraging to feel like you're slipping back a half step for every step forward. In truth, you are, but do not dwell on this. Just think of each half-step that's behind you and not the steps ahead. You might count ten steps and stop for a moment for two breaths, then take ten more. Do this until you see the light on the horizon. From this altitude, you can see the roundness of the earth. Concentrate on breathing and where you place your feet.

Around sunrise, the path seems to get steeper just before you reach the crater rim. Do not let this discourage you. This steepening means you are on the last difficult portion of the climb. It is very short. Before long, you will come to the crater rim, where it is flat and there is a well-defined and solid trail. You have made it to the top of the rim and Stella Point! This is a great success, and you will now take time to sit down, drink water, and eat snacks. If you go no farther, you have summited Kilimanjaro and earned a green certificate from the Tanzanian National Parks! It will remind you of this moment for the rest of your life.

From this spot, you can look down into the crater and see across the glaciers of the northern ice fields. Others may be resting here as well. Some will take a break for an hour or so before going back down and others will take a short break and continue on up to Uhuru Peak. The choice is yours.

For those going on, do not stop too long, or it will be very difficult to get going again. (About eight minutes is best—after that, lactic acid begins to seep into your muscles, and they will not want to climb anymore today.) Eat a little, drink water, and then get moving. On your left, you'll see white glaciers in the sun, reaching into the sky and looking like sentinels guarding a fortress. It is an amazing sight. You will want to have your camera ready to take pictures. Take care not to drop it, because your mind will not be working as well up here.

Meanwhile, keep plodding along the trail, which is not very steep. As you walk and look ahead, you'll sometimes feel like you're not moving at all, a strange illusion that happens in this area. But you are making good progress and you'll get there soon enough. It only takes about a half hour or so. As you go up the very last slight incline, you will see the famous sign at the true summit of Kilimanjaro. This is Uhuru Peak. You are just about there!

Before you know it, you'll be standing on the rooftop of Arica! You have made it! You will take your turn on the summit having your picture taken with your group or guides. You can see everything across Africa from here or from the edge of the crater. You can see the Arrow Glacier Camp far below, and the icefields that you may have seen in the IMAX movie. Be glad you did not come up that way! You might see crosses and memorials from those who have died up here, or pictures of the dead people others have brought up. If you see a bottle or a Snickers wrapper, pick it up to take back down. Think of it as a souvenir from the summit of Kilimanjaro!

If you have a GPS or a GPS watch, you can put a waypoint here to mark being at such a place. It will almost be too much for your senses. Some people sit near the summit and try to feel everything, and these thoughts can almost overwhelm you. The emotions you experience can come from the exhilaration of such a great accomplishment or for other unknown reasons that originate deep inside you. You are on holy ground for the Chagga People. You will have a gold certificate waiting for you at your ceremony in Moshi!

The Descent from the Summit

Soon enough, it will be time to go back down. This of course will be much easier. As you descend, the oxygen level will increase, and you will gain energy on the way. Some of your comrades may have stayed at Stella Point and will still be resting there and awaiting your return. You will take a few last pictures and maybe speak words of encouragement to those in other climbing groups that are still on the way up. This will help them. You will see in their faces the same difficulties and fears that you faced. Those fears will seem like they were almost a lifetime away now—or even as if they never really happened.

As you leave the crater rim, the very soft volcanic scree and small pieces of rock that were so troublesome on the way up will now be your friend. You can almost glissade down in some of these areas, taking huge steps of ten or twelve feet at a time. Be very careful not to fall on the rocks that are beside this material. Keep an eye on your fellow climbers and don't get separated from them or your guides. Below, you will see the tents of Barafu Camp. You will know that all the fears and questions of the night before, in the cold and winds, were not that bad after all.

You'll already be feeling more like yourself when you arrive at Barafu Camp, but the guides won't let you lie down to rest. They know all too well that you will never get back up if you stop now!

If you stop too long here, or lie down, this will make the rest of the day foggy and painful. To keep the good feeling you have, you must press on and get to lower altitudes. The day is far from over. From Uhuru Peak to your destination, Mweka Camp, you have 13 kilometers to go, which is roughly eight miles.

Even as you gain strength from the oxygen, you'll get weary of hiking down. This is normal. People will stop talking much and your legs will be on autopilot. This is the natural result of the small amount of sleep you had, the long climb up, and the total distance you're covering. Soon enough you'll see the welcome and familiar sight of the camp. The cooks and porters will be busy getting ready for your dinner. What a sight! It comes not a minute too soon.

You'll go through the familiar process of opening your duffel bag and setting up your personal items for the evening rest, placing everything just as it should be in your tent. You may want to fall asleep right away, and it will be hard not to, but you need to remember that you still have to eat! This is also a time when you should celebrate with others, sharing your joy with the guides, cooks, and porters. You may want to take some final pictures of your fellow travelers and staff at this last night on Kilimanjaro. Suddenly, after so much anticipation and apprehension along the way, it feels like it will be over all too soon. You'll want to experience everything you can, so you don't forget this moment in the future. It will not be long before you are asleep. Many people do not even remember eating at this camp. Often you will sleep without dreams, and then awaken from a very deep and otherworldly place as the sun begins to rise again and fill the forest with light.

In the morning, you will rise to this new day, and in some ways, a new life. You will be changed, even though your Kilimanjaro and East African adventure is far from over! You'll also find it difficult to get going, because your muscles will be very tired. But you'll know that the price for this discomfort was worth it.

After breakfast, you'll pack your personal items for the last day of hiking, down to Mweka Village. You'll be carrying a minimal amount, since you won't need much gear in the warm and moist jungle below. You'll leave your duffle by your tent one last time for the porters, and you won't see it again until Moshi. It will have more dirt on it from Kilimanjaro than it did a week ago.

During the short trip to Mweka Village—seven kilometers, four miles—you will really need your trekking poles to spare your knees. As you come to the gate, you will see many villagers awaiting your arrival. It is time to sit and have a beer or a soft drink. People will press you to look at things they have for sale. You will enjoy your visit here, which will last an hour or so. If you have a beer here, be aware that it will quickly go to your head. (Also note: the beers are very large.) Your friends and guides will keep an eye on you in case you indulge too much. You may have the Kilimanjaro song sung to you by your Tanzanian staff or others at the gate. This is a lot of fun and you should not miss it.

Before you know it, your duffel bags will be loaded on the vehicles and you'll be headed back to Moshi. There is no *pole, pole* on the way back. After walking for a week, the vehicle ride will seem very fast to you. You will not be able to get the smile off of your face. This is a fun trip, even if it is a little bit rough.

After you get back to your hotel, you'll welcome a shower as you start the process of getting the dirt and grime off your body. This will take days! The sun will probably be shining and there might be a gentle breeze blowing though the leaves of the banana trees at your hotel. You will feel like you are home in some strange way. It is time to put on clean clothes and go have a beer with your friends and fellow travelers. Maybe a hamburger with an egg on it.

The presentation ceremony of your certificates will take place at the hotel. You will visit with everybody and tip your guides; they will share the tips with everyone else. When it comes time to say goodbye to your senior climbing staff, it will seem like it all ended too quickly. This is always the case at the end of great adventures. But your trip may not be over just yet—I hope you're also planning to go on safari! Another new adventure awaits you! *Kutembea!*

CHAPTER TWENTY-EIGHT

THE MARANGU ROUTE

Horombo Camp huts on the Marangu Route in the fog.

Route Summary

Days: 6 - 7 Days (5 nights if minimum 2 nights Horombo or 6 nights with Mawenzi night or 3 at Horombo)

Length: Usually about 65 to 75 kilometers or 40 to 46 miles, depending on the exact route

Elevation Gain: Roughly 3,200 meters or 14,000 feet total, but depends on the exact route

Starting Point: Marangu Gate 1,850 meters or 6,144 feet

Camps (nights) along the way:

Mandara Hut	2,700 meters or 8,900 feet
Horombo Camp	3,700 meters or 12,200 feet
2nd Night Horombo	3,700 meters or 12,100 feet
Mawenzi (optional)	4,500 meters or 14,900 feet
Kibo Camp	4,700 meters or 15,500 feet
Horombo Camp	3,700 meters or 12,200 feet

This is the original route up the mountain, and as I said, it's sometimes called the Coca-Cola Route because it was considered the one that poor people should climb, since it was all they could afford. This is an improper name for what really is a great way up the mountain. Many people in the past chose this route because it can be done quickly—in as little as three nights before reaching the summit—but I would strongly recommend against doing that. You need extra time for proper acclimatization.

Because many people try this route as a way to save time and money, it has had a very low success rate, but if done properly, it's one of the easier and most successful routes, and it offers amazing views of Kilimanjaro. The best views are from Mawenzi Hut, which you can visit on an acclimatation day.

Many people still try to do this route too fast. You will see some of them on summit day, lying on the side of the trail passed out, or on their hands and knees vomiting violently. The only thing that will help them is descending. You may feel sorry for them, but you can't help them. You will pass them, feeling strong

5895 M
19,341 F.
UHURU PEAK
GILMAN POINT
5685 M.
18,885 F.
MARANGU ROUTE
TRAIL TO BACKSIDE
KIBO HIGH CAMP
4,700 M.
15,500 F.
MWENZI HUT
4,500 M.
14,900 F.
ZEBRA ROCK
HOROMBO CAMP
3700 M.
12,200 F.
KIFUNIKA HILL
MANDARA HUT
2700 M
8900 F.
Kilimanjaro
MARANGU GATE
1850 M   6144 F.

and ready for the summit, because you acclimatized properly on the way up. On this route, you climb about 1,000 meters (3,000 feet) every day, and it can be a pretty crowded path at times. It is the one route where you climb up and down the same trail going up and coming back down out of the park.

This has always been the most popular route, and about 40 to 50 percent of all climbers on Kilimanjaro use it. This is changing over time, as more people use routes that were not commonly traveled only a few years ago. Some people are seeking a different type of experience and prefer a route with fewer people.

In the past, climbing books have tended to heavily criticize this route because of problems created by improperly prepared climbers, unrealistic expectations, and the guidebooks themselves, which contained bad advice. This is not to say that trash and over-crowding are not real problems, but much of overcrowding on this route happened because guidebooks advertised it as a "budget" option for climbing the mountain. The Park Service is working hard to implement new policies that address these problems, but visitors and guidebooks need to do their part as well and not just add to the problems. Properly funded and prepared visitors can have a quality experience and a very good success rate on any route, including this one.

The Marangu Route is known for huts—you can't stay in tents on this one. The huts will be set up when you arrive at a camp. They're an A-frame style with dry, comfortable bunks for your sleeping pad and foam mattress. Some guide services will supply these mattresses for you.

As you know, the routes offer different views of Kilimanjaro. On the Machame Route, you walk through the Shira Plateau, and you have a very different view of Kilimanjaro than when you're coming up the Marangu, which is on a different side of the moun-tain. On the Marangu Route, you will be coming across a vast plain, or saddle, that seems like a huge desert. The views from here are remarkable.

On your way from Moshi to the Marangu Gate, you may decide to stop along the way so your cook can buy fresh meat for the trip. One of the stores is called Montana Grocery, so keep an eye out for it and other signs of village life. You will not have time to stop and visit with people on this part of the trip, though.

At the gate, there are facilities for you to use. This is a relaxed and beautiful area, and you can take a break as the last preparations are being made for your climb to begin. On the way up, after signing in with park officials at the gate, you will climb slowly though a beautiful jungle zone. Soon you will see monkeys in the trees, watching you as you walk by. They will peer at you though the branches of many thick trees and a bamboo forest.

The jungle here is thick and moist. It will be warm and humid as you climb. Look at the amazing plants and delicate flowers as you pass by. Everything seems so large in Africa— except the flowers. They are small, delicate, and vibrant.

The trail at this elevation is very good, and it will be tempting to press on quickly because the walking is so easy, but that is not the way to get to the summit! You must go *pole, pole,* even now. Soon enough you will climb above the deep jungle and into other climate zones. You will want to take in as much as you can. The climbing here will seem almost too easy, but you have hardly begun to get to the summit of Kilimanjaro.

Along the way you will take a break and have your lunch. This will be in a forested area. It's a great time to take pictures and visit with fellow travelers. Soon you will be climbing higher, and you'll see more changes to the trees and vegetation. The trees will seem to open up as you pass through them. Some of the jungle areas below were extremely dense bamboo forests, but those are behind you now. In the afternoon, you will break out into the opening at

You can see monkeys here in the jungle on the way up during the first day.

Mandara Camp. Here you'll find a series of huts and a large grassy area. Behind these are trees that tower above the camp.

These trees are often filled with colobus monkeys gliding from tree to tree. These huge black-and-white primates are really something to see. They have very long hair on their backs and tails that are white on the ends, which makes them look like they have huge white capes over their shoulders. They live most of their lives in trees and can leap as far as 50 feet through the air. They are very large creatures, but they are not dangerous to you.

In this camp, you will be assigned a hut. Each one holds four people, but they're not always full. The huts are small but quite comfortable, featuring the standard three wooden bunks along the sides, with a fourth upper bunk. You can pick your bunk and set it up any way you wish. I strongly suggest that you have an air mattress at the very least, perhaps adding a layer of foam under that. Put your sleeping bag on top of the pads and you'll be very comfortable and warm, even on cold nights. Space is tight, but there should be enough to store all your remaining gear at the foot of the bed. The bunks themselves are long enough for tall people.

A porter will bring you soap and water to clean up, and it will soon be time for dinner. Before dinner, some climbers will be taken out on a short hike that involves several hundred feet of elevation gain to an old volcanic crater, then back to camp. This is an excellent acclimatization exercise, and you should do it if it's offered. You may see blue monkeys in the trees on this trail—and as you'll see, they're shy about being photographed! It may be misty in the evening and in the mornings at this camp. During the night, if you wake up, you will likely hear animals making sounds in the forests. Some can be pretty loud at times. Don't be concerned—you're safe.

The next day, you'll get up early and have a good breakfast, getting underway on the trail around 8 A.M. This is an interesting day, because you'll be emerging from the jungle as you climb. The plants begin to change, and the country opens up quite quickly. You are on your way to Horombo Camp, and you'll get there around 4 or 5 P.M. On the way, you will pass by a holy place that I've mentioned before. It is called *Kifunika* in Swahili, and it's a spot where religious ceremonies of the Chagga are still practiced. It will be on your left as you climb.

There are many blackened trees, from the great fires that happened here decades ago. Elephants used to roam in this area, but unfortunately poachers killed them over the years. I am very hopeful that they will return someday for visitors to see again. Meanwhile, grass and flowers are growing there now, and it's a beautiful place.

Mandara Camp on the Marangu Route with four-person huts to sleep in.

As you hike up the trail, you will likely begin to feel the effects of altitude. This is common, so don't worry: it will be OK. You can walk slower, stop and drink water, or have something to eat. There is no rush. Once you get to camp, the feeling will likely pass soon enough, and remember that feeling some degree of altitude sickness at this point is not a reason to think that you won't be able to summit. Share how you're feeling with your guides, and they will help you understand this. Altitude problems are usually not very serious at this elevation. In the rare case that they are, the guides will know what to do.

When you come into Horombo Camp that evening, you will again see the familiar A-frame huts, but now in a much more open and rocky area. This is a pretty high camp—12,224 feet!— and the landscape will look very different from the forest and jungle below. It will be much cooler here, with temperatures at night often going down to freezing.

The camp is an amazing place that will seem like an international village because people from so many countries are here. Some will be happy, some won't—but you will probably be feeling well because you prepared properly and have already read this book first before coming! You will be assigned a hut and given time to clean up before dinner, which happens in the camp's great dining hall. This can be fun, and you can meet people from all around the world if you want to.

Your food will be made for you by your own cooks, so you will not be sharing food with climbers from other companies. Be prepared for a very good meal and please eat well; as you gain altitude, it's important that you take in plenty of calories. You might start with an excellent soup and bread. Then it's common practice for rice to be served with chicken or fish, sometimes beef. Vegetables and possibly mango chicken may be offered as well, you never know. Quite often you'll be served popcorn. This is how the day usually ends.

After dinner you will find the dark sky to be full of the brightest stars you have ever seen in your life. Nothing here obscures your view of the night sky. Far below the slopes of the mountain, you may see the lights of the cities. It is a remarkable sight that you will not soon forget. You might be treated to the moonrise over the East African plains, or the stars of the Southern Cross. The feeling of this place is one of wonder. It might be very cold, and you might hear the sounds of the Swahili voices of the guides and porters in their tents, drifting by you in the crisp chilly wind. Their tents will glow with colors from the lights inside, as they talk over the day's adventure. Sometimes you might hear a song.

You can now return to your hut and make sure everything is set for the morning. You will be provided with water, but remember that you should treat it again before putting it in your bottles for your hike the next day. Treating it not only once, but even twice, is a very good idea. You really need to be careful at this point.

When morning arrives it will be chilly, but it will get warm soon enough. If your guide is taking you straight to Kibo Camp from here, I think you're making a big mistake. You should be going to Mawenzi via Zebra Rocks, and then back to this camp for another night, or even two. If you do this, in the morning you'll see spectacular views of Kibo. You can even see Barafu Camp up high on Kibo from Mawenzi Hut, and you might even make out the trail to the crater rim, which you'll head for on your summit morning, a few days from now.

When people climb the Marangu Route, I believe they should spend at least one extra day at Mawenzi as a day hike. Take a look at the map and you will see that this is a separate mountain some miles to the east of the main part of Kilimanjaro. Mawenzi, at 16,890 feet, is one of the three mountains that make up what used to be Kilimanjaro. Many millions of years ago, the original Kilimanjaro collapsed into the three mountains that make up the entire geologic structure today, and you can clearly see this from Mawenzi.

Not many people actually climb up to the very top of the rocks on Mawenzi because it is very steep. They usually just hike to the base. This is where the camp is. This is a great place to have your lunch. From here you will see one of the very best views of Kilimanjaro. On the way you will have passed by a place called Zebra Rocks. They are rocks that look like they have zebra markings. It is not called this because it is a place where zebras live. Zebras do not live this high on Kilimanjaro—they are creatures of the lower plains.

Your lunch at the base of Mawenzi will be at 15,000 feet! This is very high, obviously, and it's a good idea to spend some time here—to get in as much acclimatization as possible—before going back down to Horombo Camp for the night. Rest, take a nap if you feel like it, and take in views of Kibo. Although you may experience some altitude sickness on the way here, it will pass when you sit down and take a break and eat your lunch. In all, you will climb almost 3,000 feet today before going back down to Horombo Camp for the night. It's a good workout and good preparation for your trip to the Barafu High Camp, which is at roughly the same altitude as Mawenzi.

When you return to Horombo, you'll be in the same hut and you'll be eating in the same dining hall. Take some time to relax, and keep in mind that many of those who kept going straight toward Kibo High Camp are unlikely to make it to the summit. Remember to keep up with your hydration: overall today, you should have taken in four liters of water, more if you add in the water in your food. If you didn't, drink additional water to catch up.

While you're in Horombo, you might take time to visit the caretaker of the camp. He will encourage you on your climb and maybe add that he will pray for your success and safety. Be grateful. Park employees work very hard and they don't get many days off between shifts. They can work 10 or even 20 days straight. Park caretakers in the camps are here to help you. They care very deeply about Kilimanjaro and their work.

The next night (or two nights later if you stay at Horombo Camp three nights) will be spent at Kibo High Camp. This is at about 15,500 feet, and it will likely be cold and possibly snowy. It's a desolate and windy place, but you'll get there late enough not to see much of it, and you'll be very tired anyway. Bunks are housed in a large building divided into various rooms. There's only a little time to eat—that happens in a common room—and then your main job is try and get some sleep. It can be very noisy here from

You can sleep on bunks like this one at Kibo Hut
on the Marangu and Rongai Routes.

people snoring or coughing, so ear plugs are a good idea. Do not expect a good night sleep.

Ideally, you'll be in bed by 6 P.M. or so, and you'll be back up at 11 P.M. to start a long day and your summit attempt. This is a tough period—don't expect to find people to be in a great state of mind or wanting to visit. That's OK. Everything is all about getting some rest and beginning the summit day.

Your summit morning will be the beginning of a very long day. It will be dark, cold, and probably windy. Remember that the sun will rise later and lift your spirits when it does! For now, just press on as best you can. Eat, drink, put on your warm clothes, and get started.

As always, do not concern yourself with the path ahead, just concentrate on your steps and breathing. You will stop from time to time for water and maybe a cookie, but not for long. For hours, it will seem like you're negotiating endless switchbacks and soft scree that's frustrating because you feel like you're slipping backward with each step. Just like the final route to Stella Point on the Lemosho and Machame Routes from Barafu High Camp, this small volcanic scree is pretty irritating, and each step involves slipping back a little bit. But it will pass soon enough. Keep at it!

Right about the time when you feel you've had enough, the route changes, getting pretty steep for a bit as you pass through big boulders. You are close, so don't give up now. In just a few minutes, you'll be greeted by a sign that says you're on the crater rim! What a relief! You will see the sun beginning to rise above the East African plains. It is an amazing sight that will warm your soul and give you renewed strength.

This is a good time for a break, water, and some food. You're at 18,500 feet now, less than a thousand feet from Uhuru Peak. From here it is a very gentle climb. It almost seems flat, but the true summit still looks very far away. In truth, it is not that far. You have earned a green certificate for reaching Gillman's Point. If you continue on to Uhuru Peak, you will get a gold certificate from the Tanzanian National Parks.

The last part of the hike takes about 45 minutes to an hour from here and you will pass Stella Point on the way to Uhuru Peak. It is slow, but not too difficult. Get your camera out, because there are great views in all directions. Enjoy the true summit and the famous sign that you have seen many times in books and stories. You will feel many things here, including pride in yourself for having made it, along with gratitude to the guides, porters, cooks, and fellow climbers who helped make it possible. If you see trash, pick up a piece or two and take it down.

Your day is far from over. You will go down the way you came up and continue all the way down to Horombo Camp. This is quite a walk—on summit day you'll cover more than 15 miles, with a total elevation gain of 4,000 feet—but as you descend, you'll feel the dense air and oxygen filling your lungs. Any altitude sickness you had will quickly go away. You'll pass Kibo High Camp on the way, but you'll keep going after a very short break. You can't lie down or sleep—if you do, you won't feel like continuing, so your guides will keep you on the move. There will be plenty of time to rest later in Horombo Camp.

People used to drink beer at this camp on the way back down, but not much anymore. It was always a bad idea to drink at such heights. (Besides, there will be more than enough time to enjoy great Tanzanian beer when you get back to your hotel the next afternoon.) At Horombo, relax, eat, and fall onto your bed for a very deep sleep. The next morning will seem to have arrived only moments after you shut your eyes. You will feel remarkably sharp when you wake up. Your muscles will be very tired and sore, but your mind will be clear.

Eat your breakfast and then head down the same trail you came up a few days earlier. You will enjoy this day very much, after the hard work of summiting Kilimanjaro. The pain and fears of the climb up will seem like a distant memory to you now.

The trail and the mountain will slip behind you as you approach the gate at Marangu. You'll be greeted by many climbers coming up the trail that you climbed yourself just days ago. They will have the same hopes and fears you once had. "*Jambo*," you'll say with a smile. They'll ask if you made it to the top. You'll say yes, and you'll encourage them on. That is the Tanzanian way. We are all in this together. No matter who your guide is, I will be there in spirit, and so will all our ancestors. We are all one village.

Just like when returning from the other routes, you will celebrate and get the certificate that you have earned back at your hotel. You will enjoy your first shower in a long time. Your clothes may even stand up on their own from sweat and dirt. Do not worry because there are laundry services available at most hotels that are quick and very good. Have a great dinner and visit with the other travelers. You will see new arrivals at the hotel who will notice your deep suntan and notice that you look rugged and experienced now, along with being very happy. This is all part of the fun. Tomorrow you will have a leisurely breakfast, check out of your hotel and then go onto the rest of your great journey and begin your safari!

CHAPTER TWENTY-NINE

THE MACHAME ROUTE

Entrance to the Barranco Valley on the Machame and Lemosho Routes.

Route Summary

Days: 7 Days (but you can add more days if you also camp an extra night at Shira Two or Lava Tower)

Length: Usually about 40 miles or 64 kilometers, depending on the exact route
Elevation Gain: Roughly 3,200 meters or 14,000 feet total, but depends on the exact route

Starting Point: Machame Gate 1,800 meters or 5,900 feet
Camps (nights) Along the Way (add more if you wish):

Machame Camp	3,000 meters or 9,900 feet
Shira Two	3,900 meters or 12,800 feet
Barranco Valley	3,960 meters or 13,000 feet
Karanga Valley	4,000 meters or 13,200 feet
Barafu Camp	4,600 meters or 15,200 feet
Mweka Camp	3,050 meters or 9,900 feet

Using the above itinerary will give you a very good chance of success on this route. You could make it one day shorter and skip the camp at the Karanga Valley, but I strongly urge you not to do this. You will dramatically reduce your chances of summiting Kilimanjaro, just by skipping a single day. I would even add a day or two if you can, but 6 nights/7days will work fine for most people.

Once again, many climbing operators, and even some guidebooks, have not properly informed people about this point in the past. Many are going to push the idea of doing short "budget" climbs on many Kilimanjaro routes, including this one. This is a very big mistake. In addition to reducing your chance of success, cut-rate trips can also cheat your climbing staff out of the money they need to provide for their families. With some budget climbs, unscrupulous operators may not even properly pay your guides, cooks, and porters, because the trips were too inexpensive. How much can you enjoy your trip if the good people who serve you will be victimized in such a way? Travel, trek, and climb in a fair and respectful style while you are in Tanzania!

Note: You can also go up to the Arrow Glacier from this path and attempt the Western Breach Route, but I would strongly discourage you from trying this and advise that you not book with operators who offer it.

The Route

This discussion will be relatively short, because I've already told you about most of this route in the chapter on Lemosho and Shira. From Shira Camp 2 and then up to the summit, this route is the same as Lemosho and Shira, but some books have made this confusing in the past. Basically, you should think of the Lemosho, Shira, Machame, and Umbwe routes as pretty much all the same, but with different starting points. They all come together, and they take you to the summit via the Barranco Valley and Karanga Valley Camps, then through the Barafu High Camp to Uhuru Peak. This leaves only two other fully distinct routes. These are called the Rongai—a route that has many different starting points—and the Marangu, which is totally separate, and which we have already covered. They usually go through Kibo High Camp on the night before your summit. The Northern Circuit Route is a variation of the Rongai Route, and they connect up on the back side of Kilimanjaro.

In truth, the starting points for most routes on this side of the mountain don't make all that much difference once you get past Shira Camp 2. They are unique for the first day or two, but then they come together and funnel people to a single path up the mountain. There are some additional rough, distant, unpublished, and undeveloped routes, and you can explore them if you find a guide and obtain a permit, but most routes will eventually connect you back to the three main summit trails: the Southern Circuit (Shira, Lemosho, Machame, and Umbwe), the Marangu (a single and self-contained up-and-down route) and Rongai (which also encompasses a number of entrances and the Northern Circuit). It's a good time to take a look at the maps to see how they all work.

Some of the old books will tell you there are secret routes that no one uses any longer, or ones that will take you to the summit without you having to see *any* other climbers. You will find these claims on some websites today as well.

This is not true. At best there have been some less-traveled starting points, but in the end, they always catch back up with the main summit routes I have talked about above. Additional improvements have been made to existing trails that were less-used, so they are used more often these days. You are going to see other people on your climb, no matter what you are told by an outfitter or website. The only way to climb Kilimanjaro without seeing anyone else, prior to the summit, is to go straight up the side without using a path, something that is neither feasible nor safe.

This does not mean that Kilimanjaro is not vast and wild, even on this route. It's difficult to explain just how untamed and rugged Kilimanjaro really is. It is huge, and it is marked by some of the most extreme environments in the world. You will see everything from the densest equatorial jungles near the mountain's base to high-altitude glacial snow and ice. There are plants here that live nowhere else in the world, because Kilimanjaro is so large that it has developed its own environment and endemic species. Don't be too concerned about trying to find a hidden or secret route. They do not exist, but it doesn't matter, since you will see plenty of extreme and unique places on your climb.

The Machame Route, often called the Whiskey Route (although I think we should call it by its proper name), became popular when the Marangu Route was deemed to be too crowded in the 1990s. The success rate on Marangu fell to less than 50 percent, sometimes as low as 25 percent. On the Machame Route, the success rate is more than 70 percent, and some companies have rates over 90 percent.

This low rate on Marangu—along with a significant number of injuries and fatalities—was not the fault of the Marangu Route itself, but of the explosion of people suddenly coming to climb Kilimanjaro without being adequately prepared. Tour companies and guidebooks made this situation much worse by offering or suggesting the budget trips I've mentioned, which encouraged anyone and everyone to climb Kilimanjaro. I was not kidding earlier when I told you that I recently saw a website offering to get any 50-year-old to the summit, even couch potatoes and smokers, with the site even showing what it claimed was the photo of such a client, puffing away on the top. This is nonsense and it should probably be criminal to suggest it's a good idea.

The Machame Route has always offered a significant benefit: you travel a longer overall distance to get to the top—a total of about 64 kilometers from bottom to the top and down again, compared to only 37 kilometers for the Umbwe. (In miles that's roughly 40 and 23, depending on the exact route you take and side trips.) The same is true of the Lemosho Route, and also the Shira Route, as long as you hike up the entire trail and do not use a vehicle on the first day on Shira. Time and distance will force you to acclimatize better, whether you planned it that way or not. This is what made the Machame a preferred route for several years, and it is still very popular today. The recent shift to the Lemosho Route is just a reflection of the popularity of the Machame Route, and the fact that more and more people are climbing it. But as I've said, they connect up later at Shira Camp 2. They are only different for the first two or three days.

The Machame Route also introduced people to the concept of camping in tents as opposed to staying in huts like you would on

Happy climber at the top of the crater rim above Barafu Camp.
Uhuru is just up the trail a little bit.

the Marangu Route. One is not better than the other—they are just different. Personally, I like staying in tents, and I very much like the Machame Route because of the trip past Lava Tower and into the Barranco Valley.

But not everyone likes going up the steep Great Barranco Wall the next morning. It's a challenge, for sure. But it looks much more formidable than it really is once you get on it. Another drawback to the Machame Route: it doesn't offer a lot of full-on views of Kilimanjaro, because the route itself is right on the main part of the mountain. You can't see clear views of the peak very well, though you'll see portions of the top from time to time.

Climbed properly, the route should take, at a minimum, seven days, but eight or even nine days makes more sense. I hope that, someday, all operators will commit to this longer time frame. Meanwhile, anyone who is not willing to spend this many days on the route should just stay home. Cut- rate short trips are dangerous, and they don't end up helping the local economy all that much, because inexpensive outfitters usually don't pay the local workforce properly.

Once you leave Moshi, you'll go on a beautiful ride of about 32 kilometers (a little less than one hour) that takes you to the Machame Gate. You'll see great views of village life in Tanzania, with people going about their daily business. The gate will be crowded with people coming and going, and with climbers making final preparations before they start. There are restrooms available, and you'll see equipment being weighed and loaded for porters to take up the mountain. The scene may look chaotic, but in fact it's highly organized and carefully planned.

During these preparations, last-minute changes can be made to climbing crews, and prospective employees will be waiting at the gate in case someone doesn't show up and there's an opening for a porter. People are on hand selling souvenir T-shirts, but I'd suggest that this isn't the place to buy things, because you need to watch the total weight of what you carry up the mountain.

Before you know it, your guides will call you to begin your climb! As you're well aware by now, you'll be going slow, and this is a great time to take in the remarkable jungle. Only two routes up Kilimanjaro have a jungle area as deep and heavy as this one, the other one being the Lemosho. Marangu is probably in third place. Deep dense vegetation grows all along the way here, and you will feel the moisture and thickness of it all. The various colors of dark-to-light greens, as the light tries to penetrate the dense foliage and trees, presses in around you.

You will almost feel as if you are slipping into another time and place, one that seems ancient. Soon you might look to the side and see eyes peering at you, because this place is home to monkeys and other creatures. It is so thick that you would have a hard time going very far off the trail. If you did, in a very short distance you would be hopelessly lost. But the trail is good, and you will easily find your way. Climbers in this area usually stay fairly close together, just in case, but there is nothing to worry about.

The trail soon begins to rise, and you will feel the lower parts of the deep forest begin to change around you. Trees are opening up, and you can now more easily see through the jungle. You are on your way. You can feel that the many months of training and planning are finally being put to the test! Soon enough, it will be time to stop and have lunch. As you sit there taking a break and fueling up, you will feel entranced by the surroundings. You are finally in Africa, and it is everything you thought it would be. You can take a break and snap a few photos of your fellow travelers. This is a wonderful and relaxed part of the route.

Later, as you exit the jungle and break out into the open, you'll be able to see Mount Meru, rising above the lower slopes of Kilimanjaro. This place is called Machame Camp, and it is your first camp on this route, with your tent already set up and your gear in place. To get away from the noise of camp, you might consider using a tent on the perimeter of the camp—something that usually is not difficult to do, because many people, especially on the first night, do not want a tent on the outer edge of camp. They think it's a wild place up here, and they wonder what animals might come out at night and visit their tent. This fear is misplaced; there is no danger from animals at night here. You will be safe in any tent.

Soon it will begin to get cold, but it's usually not very windy. Sometimes there is a mist that surrounds the camp. It may stay until morning, but it will burn off and the sun will warm everything during the day.

Right now, though, it's time to clean up and have dinner in a large dining tent. At this camp, you will even have chairs to sit in! This may surprise you, but you will have chairs at each dining tent on this route. Your meals will be excellent and prepared to help you take in all the calories you'll need as you climb. Your guides will keep reminding you to drink lots of water and to get in the habit of staying hydrated. This is a key to getting to the summit. You will have soup, coffee, and tea if you wish. Tea is very popular in Tanzania. We also grow some of the best coffee in the world.

In your tent, you will have a chance to visit and get to know others on your trip. Camps usually have plastic chairs for people to sit in while relaxing around the camp, not just in the dining tent. This of course depends on the operator. As I suggested earlier, most people keep a journal, and some like to read their guidebook or listen to music. At your first camp on Kilimanjaro, people will find that a journal is a good idea where it is still easy to write. It will become more difficult to think and write when you are higher up on Kilimanjaro, but it's fun to record your thoughts along the way whenever you can do so. You will be surprised to see how you wrote and what you observed along the way. It will help you to recall many things later when you get back home.

Your morning will come early, with a good breakfast and coffee or tea. If there is still a mist, it will leave soon enough. Remember that the sun will be very intense, and you do not want a sunburn at any time up here. Therefore, applying sunscreen is the first order of business, even if it's overcast in the morning. Drink lots of water and keep a number of liters of it with you on your way. You will break camp and leave your gear for the porters in your duffle bag, except for things you'll carry during the day.

The trail quickly climbs out of the last of the jungle and into an interesting zone of low brush and trees. Some sections of this trail go up the edges of canyons and old creek beds, which will

The last short climb to the top of the crater rim just before Shira Camp.

be dry during the climbing seasons. It's a beautiful area, and you might have ravens visit you on the way. The flowers are vibrant, and you will need to be careful not to touch anything that could give you a sting, no matter how pretty some of the plants are. Soon you will glimpse the summit of Kilimanjaro, but just the upper slopes. The mountain looks very big from here and the top will seem very far away.

As you climb through the rocks on the trail, the path is not difficult, but you might begin to notice the altitude. Just remember what I have taught you: stay hydrated and be sure to eat. There will be a fairly steep section later that afternoon, but it doesn't last too long. You might need a hand on some of the rocks here, but you will quickly come over the top of a rim, and then you'll go down into the Shira Plateau. You are now close to Shira Camp, which you will see in the distance. There will be many colored tents scattered in different groups. Your guides will take you to your encampment for the night.

The Shira Plateau Camp is open and a much different place from the jungle below. You may have an excellent view out the door of your tent to the top of Kibo, the main summit of Kilimanjaro. Here on Shira Camp 2, you are on one of the three summits of Kilimanjaro. As we have discussed, there was once an ancient huge volcano where Kilimanjaro sits, but it exploded—the three remaining peaks are Shira, Kibo, and Mawenzi. So, in a way, you are already on part of the top of Kilimanjaro, but not nearly so high as you will be on Uhuru Peak at the top of Kibo.

You will have a feeling of success here, since you are now well on your way. The camp is a great place to relax and really enjoy the sights as the sun sets. If you have any issues with the altitude, they will likely pass after you eat your dinner and settle in for the night. You can get a good night's sleep and be ready for the next day.

In the morning, it will usually be very bright and sunny here because there are only a few scrubby trees. The sun is even more intense at this camp and altitude, so you will be very happy you brought sunblock and a wide-brimmed hat. From here on you can expect some wind. You're much higher now, so the sunblock is crucial—this will be the case every day until you are off the mountain and in town.

This day will be different from the last couple, in that you'll be climbing at very high altitude for the first time. (Your lunch break will happen at around 15,000 feet.) You can expect to feel it, and you might even experience nausea or a headache. Not to worry. This will pass if you drink water and eat food. You will be traveling slowly and taking breaks along the way. Tell your guides how you are feeling. Take your time and do not worry if the altitude is affecting you. This is a beautiful and rugged location, with huge,

High camp at Barafu. This means snow or ice in our local language.

jagged boulders and the Lava Tower rising far above the side of Kilimanjaro.

To the left are views of Kibo, but it changes with each mile you travel. The top of this area seems very desolate, but as you continue down the trail you will enter a lush green valley that feels almost prehistoric. This is the start of the Barranco Valley. If you were feeling altitude sickness at your stop for lunch, it will quickly pass as you descend into this remarkable place.

In fact, for many people, the Barranco Valley is the best part of Kilimanjaro. At night it will freeze here, but in the day the ice melts and the waters feed a lush valley. Some of the plants curl up at night to protect themselves, but open in the day to take in the sun's warmth. Some trees have their ancient dead branches pulled tight around them like a blanket to keep them warm at night.

At the bottom of the trail is the Barranco Camp, and rising above it is the Great Barranco Wall. As we have already talked about, at first sight, it will seem very high and you will wonder how anyone can climb it. Again, don't worry: there is a path to the top, but that is for the next day. For now, just enjoy the place and settle into your tent. Your dinner is not far off. One of the classic views of Kilimanjaro can be seen from here and you will want to take a picture of it. It is not the full mountain as you might see from the Marangu Route, but it is a beautiful view of a very steep wall.

This is where the Umbwe Route connects with this path. If for some reason you can't continue, you'll take that route on the way down. But this will not be necessary for you to do, because you are well- prepared for the rest of your climb to the summit. It is a time to relax and to reflect on how far you have already come!

The rest of this route is the same as the Lemosho and Shira Routes, as described earlier. Return to those portions of the book to read about the continuation of this route as it goes along to the Karanga Valley and Barafu High Camp. The remainder your journey to the summit awaits in those pages. *Asante Sana!*

CHAPTER THIRTY

THE RONGAI/ LOITOKITOK ROUTE

The building at Kibo Hut on this route.

Route Summary

Days: 7 Days (6 or even 7 nights – use Mawenzi or Third Cave and either School Hut or Kibo Hut high camps)

Length: Usually about 40 to 55 miles or 64 to 88 kilometers, depending on the exact route
Elevation Gain: Roughly 3,200 meters or 14,000 feet total, but depends on the exact route

Starting Point: "Rongai" Gate 1,950 meters or 6,400 feet
Camps (nights – mix and match as you wish) along the way:

Simba Camp	2,700 meters or 8,900 feet
Kikelelwa Camp	3,600 meters or 11,860 feet
Mawenzi Tarn Camp	4,300 meters or 14,100 feet
Third Cave	3,900 meters or 12,800 feet
(alt) School Hut	4,700 meters or 15,400 feet
(alt) Kibo Camp	4,700 meters or 15,500 feet
Horombo Camp	3,700 meters or 12,200 feet, or out the way you came

This route is on the north side of Kilimanjaro, and it is quite different from the climbs on the southern side. There are advantages and disadvantages, and if you are interested in this route, plan carefully, because it can be a very short distance to the top if you do it with only two or three camps on the way up. You should know by now that this is not good at all. If you add enough days to the trip and do extra climbing on the side as you ascend, then it can be very safe for you. I'd recommend taking at least five to six days to get from the route's start to the top.

This is not really just the Rongai Route anymore, because they removed the gate in the actual village several years ago, but people still call the route by that name. It used to start at Rongai Village and then go up from there. It's also sometimes called Nalemoru, because the Nalemoru Forest is in this general area. (There's a path up the mountain from there as well. This route, more to the west, is called Loitokitok.) This area is on the border with Kenya,

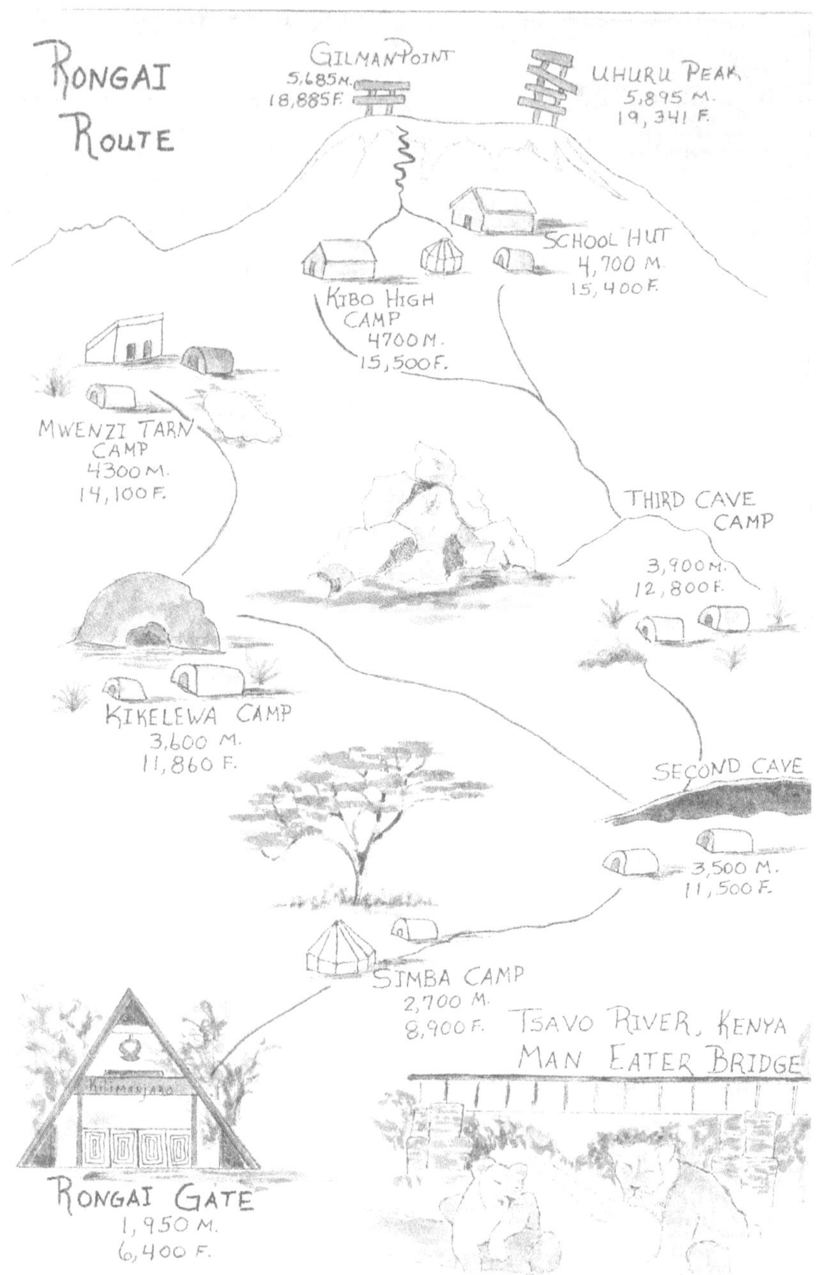
RONGAI ROUTE
GILMAN POINT
5,685 M.
18,885 F.
UHURU PEAK
5,895 M.
19,341 F.
SCHOOL HUT
4,700 M.
15,400 F.
KIBO HIGH CAMP
4700 M.
15,500 F.
MWENZI TARN CAMP
4300 M.
14,100 F.
THIRD CAVE CAMP
3,900 M.
12,800 F.
KIKELEWA CAMP
3,600 M.
11,860 F.
SECOND CAVE
3,500 M.
11,500 F.
SIMBA CAMP
2,700 M.
8,900 F.
TSAVO RIVER, KENYA
MAN EATER BRIDGE
KILIMANJARO
RONGAI GATE
1,950 M.
6,400 F.

which is where Rongai Village is located. In the past, the road here was pretty rough, but today it is good for the most part. It no longer takes you the better part of a day to get here.

There is an official gate where you will begin your climb, just like at Marangu or Machame. There is no store. You can visit the villages, but there are no stores or villages right by this new gate.

What changed this original area was logging, which has been going on in the surrounding forests for a long time. The trees here, mostly pine, are used for furniture. Many people built modern wooden houses, and then the people said, "We will have to move this place." That is why the old gate is gone and the Tanzanian National Park Service moved it to this new location. Animals also have a tendency to leave an area after it has been logged, and when new wooden houses are built. You will not see the animals that were there in the past.

Some years ago, we would take climbers on this route, and you almost felt like you had all of Kilimanjaro to yourself. You could go a long time and never see any others. People didn't like the rough drive to get to the start of the climb, which is another reason why people started coming here less often. Then, starting roughly ten years ago, two things happened. First, the road got much better—it's now smoother—but even more important, people began hearing about this route and that it wasn't crowded.

As climbing Kilimanjaro became more popular, people tried to find "new" routes where there were not so many climbers. You will not likely have this route to yourself today, though. It is definitely gaining in popularity. At the same time, the Tanzanian National Parks are doing a great job of trying to make all the routes better for climbers and trekkers. New rules and facilities are making a big difference. No one could have imagined that the changes would happen so fast on Kilimanjaro, and that the number of people coming here would grow so quickly. This route is a good option today, but people do it differently now, and you should as well. When I say differently, I mean that they are taking much longer to do this climb and spending time on side-hikes, like to Mawenzi Tarn Hut.

I would very strongly suggest that if you are considering this side of the mountain, that you plan on visiting and spending some time at Mawenzi. This is a great way to make it a better, safer, and much more interesting trip as well!

The Tsavo River Bridge

Just so you know, a lion can and will eat a person sometimes. Back in 1898, the British were building a bridge over the Tsavo River for a railroad going to Uganda, another East African country. Several thousand workers were brought here from India to build it. They also built a railroad bridge in Kenya, not all that far from present day Rongai, which is just inside Tanzania. This project was done during the bad colonial times, when foreign invaders abused the people, the land, and the native cultures. Such imbalances are bad for everything. It was a dark period.

One day, two lions began to eat the people who were working on the bridge. Why did this happen? No one can really say for sure, but I think it can happen when people disrespect nature and the balance of things. It is a mistake to do so.

The lions kept eating people each evening. The workers tried starting big fires at night, and they also built walls of branches with thorns to keep the lions out. It did not work. The lions would drag the workers from their tents at night and devour them. The workers were very afraid. It's said that the lions ate 135 people before they were killed by a hunter; the lions tried to kill the hunter as well. The skulls and skins of these lions were taken to America. You can see them on display at a museum in Chicago. These lions did not have manes, but they were males.

I think that nature needs a balance, and when you disturb it, bad things can happen. People must respect the history, nature, and culture that have been around for a very long time. It is a bad idea to fail to do so.

If you come to Tanzania to climb this side of Kilimanjaro, you will remember this history of the man-eating lions of the Tsavo River. Even today, the bridge over the Tsavo River at this location is called Man-Eater Bridge.

Simba Today

I have told you this story so you will know the history of this area, but in truth, a lion will not eat you these days. However, the first camp on this route is called Simba Camp! Simba is Swahili for lion. It is called that because people do see lions here, but not very often. You will not need a gun or a guide with a weapon.

In fact, there are not many animals of any kind left along this route anymore. There are cliffs where you might see antelope, and from time to time some buffalo, but very seldom will you see lions. I have only seen a couple at a far distance over the years here. Still, because of the name, some of the porters get worried. They also know the stories. But you will be safe from lions. This area is very dry most of the year, which is another reason that animals don't come here often anymore. It will almost always be dry when people are climbing.

As I have said, your first camp is Simba. There is a jungle here, but not like the jungle on the southern side of Kilimanjaro, where the forests are very thick, deep, and full. Because there is less vegetation, there can be some good views of Kibo and the northern ice fields from this route.

Moving up from Simba Camp, you will go to Second Camp. It has no Swahili name, because it was not a traditional location for tribal people. You will find this to be a desolate and dry place, and I mean *really* dry. There are some plants here, like juniper and olive trees, that can exist without water for very long periods of time. You will see very few of the magical plants that are found in the Barranco Valley or other areas on the southern side of Kilimanjaro where there is more moisture.

That said, Second Camp has some interesting features. I have always felt this to be a wild place, and it seems very different from anywhere else on Kilimanjaro. I think it has a beauty all its own. Second Camp is also a junction from which you can go off in a number of different directions. Water is often an issue in this area, and your porters may have to carry it for a long distance, depending on conditions. You will see many stream beds along the way, but if you're in climbing season, they will most often be dry or close to it. If they are full of water, then you probably made a big mistake and are climbing at the wrong time of year!

Along the way you will pass a series of caves. You may even have lunch near one of them. People used to camp in them. In the past, there were many campfires that left smoke on the roof of the caves, but today it is not legal to camp in them. There are a number of routes from here that you can take, depending on how you booked your trip. You can go to the School Hut and then on to Kibo Hut, or to the Mawenzi Tarn Hut or out across to the saddle between Mawenzi and Kibo. You can also stay at the Kikelewa Campsite on the way. Most books seem to make this confusing to the reader, so I will explain it a different way.

In the end, you are always going to the same place. You will head to the crater rim and then on to Uhuru Peak, no matter which path you take to get there. You can reach it from a number of locations, but that has more to do with planning and working

A side trip to Mawenzi Hut is a great idea to adjust to the altitude.
It is a good place to spend some time and eat your lunch.

with your guide or guiding service ahead of time, discussing the logistics of what they offer and how much time you will spend to safely acclimatize. I do not think it makes a lot of difference which camps you stay at when coming from this direction. You have options. There is no best or perfect route. I tend to like the Mawenzi views and I will explain them more in detail, but this is not the only way.

What *is* important is that you do not climb too high all at once. This will make you sick. Think over the profile of your climb and try, each day, to climb a reasonable distance to a reasonable altitude, and then go back to camp. It is always good to climb high and sleep low, so find a way to climb a bit higher and then go back down to your camp for the night and your rest. You will sleep much better and keep your acclimatization going properly. Rather than try to understand everything about these camps, talk to people who have climbed this route and to your guides. Find a plan that works for you. From here it can be very smart to go to Mawenzi. No matter which camps you use, take the time to explore and let your body adjust to the changes in altitude.

If you decide to go to another camp and spend some extra days and time along the way, you will be richly rewarded with some of the best views of Kilimanjaro! Remember how I said that there are some advantages of this route? Well, one of them is the truly amazing view from Mawenzi, looking back across the plain. Mawenzi Tarn (tarn means mountain lake, and there is one here) has a hut, and it gives you the chance to climb up and see across to one of the very best views of Kibo, home to Uhuru Peak. Some people enjoy this view so much that they want to stay longer. It is a great place to relax for the day, or even two.

You can also see, in the distance, the two climbing routes to the crater rim at Stella Point and Gillman Point. They are small from here and you can just barely make them out. Then you can imagine yourself leaving Barafu or Kibo High Camps and making your way up to the crater rim on summit day. I do not know why, but visualizing this can help people feel like they will make it to the summit. Maybe this is because they have now seen it with their owns eyes. Make no mistake, it is still a very long way off, but you can see the whole route to the top from this one place.

You should now read the section on the Marangu Route, which discusses the climb from the Kibo High Camp to the summit. The higher parts of the climb will be very similar on this route. Remember that there are only two routes to the summit that I recommend. They are the same no matter where you come from down below. In the past, books have made this difficult to understand. They are via Barafu High Camp and Kibo High

Camp. There is a third route up the Western Breach, and a few others I will not even mention here, but you should not climb any of them. They are not safe for the average climber.

I think it is better to just think of all of these camps from the Rongai area as part of the northern routes up Kilimanjaro, via the general Rongai Route, even though the path no longer goes through Rongai Village and there are multiple starting points in the general area. The path from this area is much shorter, but you can spend more of your days relaxing and exploring the other camps in the area as day hikes, or you can consider going to Mawenzi and spending some time there. The short distances on these sections of the trails leave a lot more time each day for wandering around and relaxing.

If you wish, you can go the other direction to the School Hut, not too far from Kibo High Camp. This used to be called the Outward Bound Hut some years ago. You may still see it referred to this way in some guidebooks, but it is not called that today. This is also a way to the summit, via that path. You can camp here and summit from here, but not without adding some time to your climb in the morning on summit day.

I really think that Mawenzi is better because of the additional days, even though it is longer. The climb from School Hut joins up with the route from Kibo High Camp Hut on summit morning. There is not a lot to see in this area, and it is tough on summit day. The other benefit of Mawenzi, as opposed to the extra day at School Hut, is that you will have plenty of time to explore around Mawenzi while staying there. It is a good idea to climb a bit higher to make your night more comfortable when you go to sleep. There are a couple of buildings at Mawenzi, but you will not stay in them. You will camp in tents for a night if this is your preference. There is a lot to see here, with some of the very best views anywhere of Kilimanjaro!

Here is the final part of the climb just before Uhuru Peak on this route.

When you are done with your summit, you can climb down via the Marangu Route, and if you do, you may end up staying in the huts at Horombo Camp on your descent. From here, you will also be going down through the dense green jungle and forest areas below Mandara Camp. This can make up for missing much of the jungle on your climb up from the northern side of Kilimanjaro, via the Rongai Route. If you come down this way, you will pass by the jungle much more quickly than you would have done on the way up.

In summary: It is a longer drive to get to the start of your climb in this area. It will usually be very dry during the climbing season. There is less vegetation on this route, and the jungle or forest areas are much sparser. There is far less water most of the time. There are multiple camping sites available and a number of options here for ways to spend extra days. There are some of the very best views of any route on Kilimanjaro. There used to be more animals here, but various factors changed that, from logging and development to climate change. You will not likely see as many climbers on this route as you will on Marangu or Machame. You may be in a combination of tents and huts on your climb.

CHAPTER THIRTY-ONE

THE NORTHERN CIRCUIT ROUTE

You have made it! You are standing on the very top of Kilimanjaro!

This is the last route for you to consider on Kilimanjaro. I am not putting in a specific itinerary for this route, but I am adding a map for general orientation. If I did put in a specific itinerary, it would use Shira or Lemosho as the starting point and Moir Hut as a waypoint. Just like most of the others, it is a combination and shares some portions of the trail and your summit day with other routes. It is by far the wildest and least-used trail on Kilimanjaro, and it will likely stay that way for a number of reasons. I do not consider this to be a traditional route up the mountain, and it's not for everyone. But if you're fit and like challenging experiences, it's certainly a memorable choice.

The Northern Circuit Route begins at the Shira or Lemosho Gate and then continues along the entire northern side of Kilimanjaro, eventually joining up with portions of the Rongai Route. Think carefully over my advice on the Shira starting point and make sure you begin at a lower "Shira" altitude (there is more than one place to begin), even if it means climbing not far from a road for a day. Do not start your climb at 11,800 feet by driving in a vehicle to get there! If you do this, you will likely get sick and not enjoy your climb as much, or in some cases even end your climb far too quickly. Try to begin your climb at Shira near a similar altitude as the Lemosho Gate, or not more than 1,000 feet above that elevation.

On this route, you will probably camp on nights one and two at the Simba and Moir Huts, which are established camps. Beyond that, there are not the same types of established camp locations like on the other routes until you get most of the way around the northern side. I have added one for the map that people call Buffalo, but not everyone uses this location. In truth, you can select many different camps to make this route work and companies will offer a number of different options. Some companies can even make their own camps along the way as well and they will work fine.

After Moir or especially after Buffalo, the route becomes very wild. It's a long trek and there are few facilities as you climb up and down for a number of days. The camping spots are unremarkable,

NORTHERN CIRCUIT
4.020M BUFFALO 13,188Ft CAMP
THIRD CAVE CAMP 3.900M 12,800Ft
MOIR HUT
SCHool Hut
UHURU 5,895M PEAK 19,341Ft
4,200M 13,800Ft
4,700M 15,400Ft
MAWENZI TARN HUT 4,300M 1,4100 Ft
SHIRA #2 3,550M 11,600Ft
KIBO HIGH CAMP 4,700M 15,500Ft
DESCENT ROUTE
SIMBA CAMP 3,600M 11,800Ft
HOROMBO HUT 3,700M 12,100Ft
SHIRA ENTERANCE
KILIMANJARO
MARANGU GATE 1,850 M 6,140 Ft

and most people consider this to be a lonely place all along the way. I agree. One of the greatest dangers of this route is that, because it is so long on the northern side of the mountain between established trials off of Kilimanjaro, you do not have easy options for leaving the mountain. If you get sick or injured, there's no quick way down. In this regard, it is very different from the other routes.

On most of the routes up Kilimanjaro, you can return to lower altitudes and be on your way out of the park in a single day. On the northern circuit route, that process can take two days or more. You might have to climb higher to get off the mountain. If you are very sick this may not be possible.

Another issue is that if you are not feeling well at Moir Hut, you will be faced with a difficult decision about going forward into this long, desolate zone. This could force you to turn around when your condition might have gotten better on another route with more options.

You won't find much water on this route. This side of Kilimanjaro is very dry most of the year. There are few animals here. You might see some elands or cape buffaloes. The vegetation and trees are sparse, nothing like what exists on the south side of the mountain. The water you find will be very precious and you cannot waste any of it. You will definitely need to treat it properly before drinking it. Don't expect to be drinking clear water in many areas on this route—unless someone carries it there. This does not make it unsafe, because it will have to be treated, but it does not look great at times.

The positives are that you will get some excellent views of the mountain. The ice fields on the top can be seen from many locations along this route. As you traverse the northern side of the mountain, you will actually be traveling farther north and away from the peak for a while. You will be in some places that are so wild that you will have to scramble through rocks in places where the trail is hard to discern. The camps are very rustic.

You won't see a lot of other trekkers. Another positive is that, most days, you will be climbing up and back down successive small valleys. This can really be a benefit with your acclimatization and your eventual summit day success. If you do climb this route, you probably will do well once you reach Uhuru Peak, thanks to the time you've spent on the trail, the distance you've covered, and the constant elevation changes.

After you traverse the northern side of Kilimanjaro on this path, you will end up going to School Hut or Kibo High Camp and then on to the summit. If you added in a side trip to Mawenzi, this journey would be very long, but you would likely be very successful on summit day.

This route will take you between eight to ten days to do successfully, perhaps more. If you don't mind the length and the issue of being so far from rescue, it can be a very good rustic, private climb of Kilimanjaro. You would need to do extra preparation for this route and be in the best condition of your life to consider climbing it. I would strongly suggest that you only book such a trip with a guide service and lead guide who have done it a number of times. This is not a route for an inexperienced lead guide. You will also need extra porters to carry additional water and supplies at times, depending on water availability.

It will be difficult to find individual people to talk to who have climbed this route. It's a route that is more for people who are looking for something quite different from the rest of the climbs. Something very wild and remote. I would begin by talking to a number of climbing operators who have done it in the past and offer it as an option. Check for references from long-established hotels in Tanzania. It is possible that more operators will offer this

Here is the high country on Mawenzi. It is very rugged and beautiful up higher.

trek in the future, and it could become more popular, but I doubt it will ever become all that crowded.

If you can find some operators who guide this route, make sure to get references, and then reach out to the climbers who went on this route and talk to them. Remember that operators are not likely to give you the names and contact information of people who were not successful or did not like it. That is OK. Even talking to successful climbers can tell you a lot about their expectations and experiences. This side of Kilimanjaro does not feature any serious objective hazards or any steep areas to climb like some other routes do. Nothing should eat you in your tent at night either, even though it is a very wild place. Animals are not an issue, here and you will not need a ranger with a gun to protect you.

In summary, the main negative will be the distance required to get back out of the park from some of the more remote portions of this trail in the event of problems. The positives are the distance, solitude, and increased chances of making the summit because of strong acclimatization.

CHAPTER THIRTY-TWO

CRIME, GUNS & SAFETY ON KILIMANJARO & IN TANZANIA

Climbers can feel very safe as they travel along the slopes of Kilimanjaro.

The process of getting a permit to own a gun in Tanzania is very long and drawn-out. Among Tanzanians, it's usually wealthier people who want to buy a gun—they think they need protection from criminals—but the government makes the process complicated and difficult. The goal is to ensure that permit holders really know how to use a gun, how to take care of it, and how to store it safely and properly. That is, in the very rare case that private citizens will be allowed to own a gun in the first place.

You see, in Tanzania, we believe that we must all be safe, and that no one without training and knowledge should have a gun. The gun must be securely stored so that other people can't be injured. The government will teach citizens how to use a gun if they're involved in some way with national service, but before they'll allow you to own one as a private person, you have to demonstrate that you know what you're doing. They'll also assess your mental state to decide if it's safe for you to possess a firearm to begin with.

As a result of such regulations, very few people own a gun in Tanzania, and people here are fine with that. We have a peaceful and prosperous culture. If people know you have a gun in your house, many will not even come by to visit you.

We believe that guns create all kinds of violence in a society. If you have a gun, and a thief comes to your house, then the thief may decide he has to kill you because he knows you have that gun. Perhaps you would have lost some property during a burglary, but now you could lose your life because you're armed. This is very foolish. People in Tanzania know that a gun does not make you safe.

We believe this is the civilized way for a country to keep from having the constant senseless acts of gun violence and crime that can be seen in other parts of the world. Our policies also make things safer for you as a visitor. Guns are not banned, but they are strictly controlled to keep everyone, both citizens and visitors, safe. In many parts of the world where guns are prevalent, visitors understandably feel unsafe. In countries where there are lots of guns, you might get robbed or killed by somebody who has one, but that is very unlikely to happen in Tanzania. We have a very low crime rate against tourists, and visitors can feel very safe because of this. Shootings are very rare in Tanzania.

In planning your trip, whatever else you do, do not bring a gun of any kind into our country, for any reason. You will not need one for protection and it is illegal to have.

As a guide, I have seen people try to smuggle weapons into the country. This is a bad idea, and it will not end well for you—in fact, it will ruin your trip. You will likely be reported to the authorities and they will take action. To them, this is a grave matter, and it's a growing problem because people in some countries are buying so many guns these days.

Some people have also come to Kilimanjaro with huge knives. You do not need one for protection! Do you think you will kill an elephant or a leopard with your knife? I can assure you that you won't need it.

In some areas where you'll travel, you'll see that National Park Rangers have weapons. They're armed to keep order—primarily against poachers—and to protect you, usually from wild animals that might pose a risk. The best way to stay safe in wild areas is to simply trust and listen to your guides, especially on safari. Visitors are rarely injured by large animals like a lion or a hippo. On Kilimanjaro itself, there is almost no risk to climbers and trekkers from wild animals, and injuries to visitors and climbers in this area are extremely rare.

As for other types of crimes in Tanzania and on Kilimanjaro, it would be very unusual for a client to have something stolen from them on the mountain today. We have very good communications, and we stay in touch with the rangers. We can get assistance quickly if we see anything suspicious. Serious incidents usually involve someone who is sick or needs medical attention. There is seldom any other type of safety problem.

It's also helpful that we have many more rangers on the trails these days. It depends on the company, but many of the guides now have radios so they can talk directly to the Park Service and the rangers in case there's a problem, or if they need information or help on a rescue. It's a good idea to book with a guide service or company that has a radio, so they can stay in touch with the rangers. I would be concerned if a company did not have this type of communication system.

Another benefit from technology these days: there is cell phone reception on many portions of the mountain now. As recently as ten years ago, there wasn't much coverage at all. These days, as much as 70 percent of the mountain has coverage, and that figure keeps growing. Coverage is still difficult to get on the northern side of Kilimanjaro—where the Northern Circuit Trail is—so keep that in mind.

On the subject of cell phones: I don't understand why somebody would come all the way to Kilimanjaro and then try to get coverage so they can do some work with their office back home. This is not a good idea; it amazes me that people want distractions with technology when they are in such a wild and beautiful place. I think this is sad. Be respectful to this place and to others by leaving your work at home. It will be there when you get back.

Sometimes we have seen poachers on the trail whose aim is to steal honey from bees, and we always make sure our clients keep a long distance away from them. We might take pictures of them for the rangers, but we never want to get too close when poaching is happening. Often the poachers will use smoke to get bees to leave their hives, but this practice has been very dangerous in the past, since some poachers have started large wildfires It's really unusual to see poachers these days. The rangers watch for them carefully all the time.

Another problem in the old days was that poachers would steal things from clients' tents, but that—along with poaching of big animals like elephants or antelope—is extremely uncommon now.

You will not find much crime in the rest of Tanzania, though there are pickpockets in some of the bigger towns. It's really not all that common, but it's smart to protect your personal items, cash, and important papers.

You can help by being safe and responsible, especially when traveling in larger cities. Secure your money and important documents, and think of using a money belt to wear inside your clothes as a place for your valuables. You should also secure your luggage or travel bags with a lock that airport security can open with a government security key. All travel stores who handle travel bags or suitcases will sell these types of locks.

CHAPTER THIRTY-THREE

ALCOHOL, MARIJUANA & DRUGS ON KILIMANJARO

These climbers are smart because they are celebrating back
at Mweka Village instead of on the summit.

The guides do not like clients to bring alcohol on the mountain.
That said, a lot of clients do it anyway, because they want to have
a drink to celebrate reaching the summit. They also like to drink

inside their tents in the evening to relax. It's not easy for us to keep track of everything a client might bring on the trip, but we definitely think it's a bad idea to bring alcohol for any reason.

One of the biggest dangers is that alcohol makes people dehydrated. You may not have thought about this, but dehydration can cause serious risks as you climb to higher altitudes. It can also change your blood sugar and cause other serious problems at altitude. Lowering your blood sugar while climbing can result in mental confusion as well. You can lose energy, and then you might fall and injure yourself. Any injury at high altitude can be quite serious, even fatal. The higher you go, the more the risks compound.

Alcohol makes you dramatically drunker when you're at high altitude than you would be at lower altitude. I have even seen some people go crazy when they drank at high-altitude or on the summit. I have seen porters who decided to drink at high altitude go nuts and start shouting at people. Porters who do this are never hired again.

We've had people who smuggled alcohol and drank it at night and then found they couldn't sleep. You will likely have some difficulties sleeping at higher altitudes anyway, and you need all the sleep you can get—it's very important for the success of your climb and your summit bid. I've had clients go crazy and try to run down the mountain because they panicked after drinking alcohol in the evenings. Panic is a common reaction: the effect of alcohol is so much stronger at altitude that your behavior cannot be predicted. It may not be like anything you have experienced in the past when drinking.

I've also had problems with Western guides who came with a group and drank alcohol and used nicotine on the mountain. It's not always easy to catch them doing this, because they're careful to hide it. There are times when they have small parties inside tents, in which clients and Western guides start drinking, then stay up all night talking and don't sleep. This creates risks from immediate fatigue the next day and from chronic fatigue over time. Another problem: when people drink at higher altitudes, they can suddenly feel too warm, so they decide to take their clothes off. You do not want to behave irrationally on Kilimanjaro. You could embarrass yourself or ruin the trip for others.

Unfortunately, a lot of people—including some guides and porters—smoke marijuana on the mountain, though this seems to be less common than it used to be. But it still happens, and my warning is the same: using any recreational drugs or alcohol is a bad idea.

Some people in Tanzania smoke cigarettes, and smoking is a fairly common sight on the slopes around Kilimanjaro. Men smoke more often than women, and I'd say that probably 20 to 30 percent of the population in this part of Tanzania smokes cigarettes. But smoking is not good, especially on the mountain, where you need healthy lungs that take in a lot of oxygen.

When I have clients who smoke, I tell them at the briefing that they need to stop smoking for the week. Of course, it's impossible to stop them completely. I do the best I can to describe the dangers of using cigarettes while they are on the climb, noting that it will be much harder for them to breathe and get oxygen in their lungs when they need it most. Then I tell them that once we are back off the mountain, they can smoke again if they want to. You might find your planning and fitness program to be an excellent time to quit smoking before you come here! Then you can celebrate your success in quitting by summiting Kilimanjaro and reaching Uhuru Peak!

We are finding that more and more people come to the mountain and bring nicotine chewing gum or lozenges. Then they don't need to smoke cigarettes while they're climbing. It seems like a good thing: we see fewer clients actually smoking cigarettes when they have this option available. Honestly, though, I think it's a better idea not to use *any* drugs, including nicotine, on your climb. I don't think it's as bad for people to use chewing gum or lozenges for nicotine rather than smoking cigarettes, but you're better off climbing clean.

As for any other types of illegal drugs, do not even think of coming if you would bring something like that to Tanzania. For one thing, you might be prosecuted for possessing these substances. I am sure you would not like to go to jail in Tanzania. On the mountain, you would be very unsafe and pose a risk to the others who might have to rescue you. If you are reading this book, such an idea has not likely even entered your mind. It is good for people to understand this ahead of time so they can share this information with others.

If you bring prescription drugs on your trip, which of course many people do, it's a good idea to keep a copy of your prescriptions with you, among your important documents. This is in case someone at customs, or at your airport on your return, questions you about them. My point in bringing this up again is so that you can prove that any drugs in your possession are lawful ones.

CHAPTER THIRTY-FOUR

PARTIES, ESPRESSO & FUNERALS ON UHURU PEAK

Kilimanjaro is a sacred and Holy mountain for us.
I hope you respect our land and our culture.

As I have previously told you, when people come to the mountain, we're going to weigh everything that a client wants to have on Kilimanjaro. If they're bringing too much weight, we'll require them to remove some things and leave them behind. Proper planning ahead of time will make this process go much smoother.

Some people don't want to take anything out of their duffle bag for the climb, which means we have to go through the items with them one by one. We tell them they can only have 20 kilograms of weight in the duffel and that's it.

You'd be amazed at what people want to bring. I've had some clients who brought their entire espresso machine, so they could make fresh coffee on the mountain. They hired extra porters to carry all the extra coffee equipment, coffee grounds, and even solar-powered charging panels so they could recharge the batteries that run the machine. All this so they could make fresh coffee at 19,341 feet above sea level. In some ways, I have to admit, it was fun. Their hope was to make fresh coffee for everyone else on the trip, including the guides and porters. And this was throughout the entire trek, not just as a stunt on the summit. Everyone liked the coffee very much, but I would not recommend that you try to do this! The guys who did it came from South Africa.

Sometimes people bring large photographs of family members who have died, and they also bring the ashes of these dead people. Their hope is to take these up to the top of the mountain. A surprising number of people decide to honor their dead relatives in this way.

Of course, this practice can lead to problems. When we are cleaning up trash on the mountain, we find—you guessed it— many pictures of dead relatives. People like to put them near or on the signboards at the summit. This is not a good idea, because they're not going to stay mounted in place after being exposed to wind, rain, and sun. We also have to remove them when they are posted there. Ones we miss are destroyed, and pieces of these photos are blown all over the mountain. Then we have to pick up what's left, pack it out, and dispose of it as trash.

Some people just leave the photos alongside the trail if they can't make it to the summit. These photos and ashes won't last on the trail, either, and this is not a good or proper memorial—it's disrespectful to the mountain, to the other climbers, and to our culture. I don't know why people do this, but I assume it must have to do with their religious beliefs. Maybe these people believe that they are closer to their God on top of Kilimanjaro, so it's easy for them to get the message to whatever deity they believe in. Maybe so, but please do not do it here. Perhaps you could just say a prayer, instead.

The National Park Service does not seem to care about people bringing up ashes, but they don't like all the pictures and trash being left there. The Park Service makes us keep the mountain clean, so it's a problem for us as guides. It's hard enough to get up Kilimanjaro and safely off it again with our clients. We don't want to have to haul out more weight, and a lot of the trash we remove from the summit is pictures of dead people.

It's disrespectful to leave anything of any kind on the summit of Kilimanjaro. No one else wants to see it. If all the memorials and other mementos that were left were still there now, you couldn't even walk through the area. It would be like a huge garbage dump. Please do not do it.

Clients also bring alcohol to the summit. These days, we find a lot of bottles of wine and champagne that people drank and left behind, carelessly discarding the empty bottles. The guides have to clean these up and haul them down—and they're heavy, so it's not fair and it's not kind. It seems that people from all different cultures do this; the problem isn't confined to one particular country. Often, once people have had their drink, they will simply throw the bottle away. Sometimes it hits a rock and breaks. This is very sad to see and tough to clean up.

The problems are bad enough that guides have been talking to the Park Service about compensating us when we bring trash down. It would be best if no one left anything on the mountain or everyone hauled out their own trash.

So here's my request: please do not plan a funeral, memorial service, or any other such event or party on the summit. Do not plan to drink with your friends on the summit. If you do, pack everything out, and watch for any other trash that someone else might have left.

CHAPTER THIRTY-FIVE

WHAT *NOT* TO DO ON KILIMANJARO

Classic view of Kilimanjaro between Barranco Camp and the Karanga Valley.

Some people have done pretty strange things on the mountain, and as I think you've gathered, I usually don't approve of these ideas. I've had people who wanted to parachute down from the top.

The parachutes usually don't work right because the air is so much thinner, and the parachutists end up falling onto the rocks and getting injured. This is a bad idea and it usually ends poorly, sometimes leading to serious accidents. It is disrespectful to the other clients on Kilimanjaro and to our local culture and religion as well.

You will have to get a special permit if you want to do something dumb like this. The Park Service will require you to get extra insurance to pay for a helicopter rescue prior to even attempting such things. The helicopter insurance is very expensive, and since these stunts serve no purpose and can put other people's lives at risk, pursuing them is reckless and selfish.

Another problem we have these days is that individuals will come with a group, then they decide they don't want to stay with that group, so they take off on their own. This makes things very difficult for the guides, and it's unsafe for many reasons. If there are ten people and a couple of them want to walk faster and break away from the group, then others get left behind. We need to be able to keep an eye on the whole group to keep them safe.

When clients want to go faster, they start to become a little crazy about going fast and getting to the summit ahead of everybody else. The funny part is that the very people who are in such a hurry will generally fare worse, decreasing the likelihood of ever getting to the summit. Most of the climbers who started walking faster at lower elevations generally never make it to the top. The others, who walked more slowly down below—as they were told to do—pass them at some point higher on the mountain and have a great summit day. The people who were in such a hurry often break down near the top. We see them on summit day, still far away from completing the climb, on all fours, throwing up, or even passed out on the side of the trail.

Most people are fine to deal with, but every once in a while, we get a client who won't listen and who wants to argue and complain.

Sometimes we get people who want to debate distances—how far they've gone, how far away things are—because they're reading about it on their GPS watch or in a guidebook. The guides know where they are and where they're going. Bickering with them about these things wastes time; it makes no sense. The guides are very experienced on the mountain, and it doesn't really matter what your watch, your GPS, or a guidebook says to you.

Believe it or not, we've even had a few clients who wanted to fight each other over things like this—one time we had to call in a Park Ranger to resolve the issue. To put it mildly, you don't want a person like this on your trip. You can avoid it by making sure, in advance, that the people in your group are good-natured, aren't prone to complaining, and understand what it means to climb as part of a team. Get to know your group before coming here. If possible, do some hikes or backpacking trips with them in advance.

It's important to always remember that even if you bring a Western guide to accompany you, you still must have a local Tanzanian guide. This is a good rule, because sometimes we even have problems with Western guides. This usually occurs on the night before summit day. When you set out in the morning, it will be dark, and you have to know exactly where to go to be safe when making your way through the rocks during the final stages of the climb, just before the crater rim. Sometimes Western guides will want to take the lead that day, but they don't know the right way to go, which they think they do because they have a GPS. But it's not the same thing—what your GPS says is no match for what an experienced guide knows.

We do not want to have to turn around and go around rocks that are too difficult for the clients to get through because their guide went the wrong way. On summit day near the top, safe route-finding is difficult unless you know the exact way to go, and thanks to their experience, the local guides always do.

It's extremely important that the clients understand that, even if they have a Western guide, they must follow the instructions of the Tanzanian guides—on summit morning in particular. They are very experienced on the mountain and they will be much better at assessing when it's time to stop a client to make sure they drink some water or eat some food. They have years of experience in seeing the symptoms of people who might be developing a serious problem. The Western guides may not understand this as well, so it's very important to have a good relationship with everyone and listen carefully to the Tanzanian guides.

Although it's OK for people to bring iPods or other things to listen to on the trail, it's important that you not use them on summit day. You have to listen for ice fall and rockfall in some places. You need to be able to hear your guides very clearly. You also need to hear the wind. Listening to music is fine for chilling out in your tent, or even in the mess tent. But when you're trekking, the most important thing is safety.

To review, here are the main things to remember about how to behave on the mountain:

*Listen to your guides

*Walk slowly

*Don't leave others in your group behind or go out ahead

*Be patient

*Be respectful of others

*Follow the instructions of the local guides very carefully on summit day

*Don't bring alcohol or drugs to the summit

*Don't endanger others who might have to rescue you by being foolish

CHAPTER THIRTY-SIX

LEAVING NO TRACE ON KILIMANJARO

This is a view of Horombo Camp with clouds below on a nice day.

Kilimanjaro has seen increasing problems with plastic bags and water bottles. The Park Service has now banned disposable water bottles on the mountain, so you shouldn't buy those in town and plan to carry them on a climb. This is a very good development! You should plan, even from home, to bring proper refillable drinking containers when you come over.

We don't see people bringing cans of soft drinks very often, but we do get a lot of candy wrappers and various kinds of plastic packaging. Some people just throw them on the side of the trail, and the guides and porters have to pick them up. Probably the most popular candy bar is Snickers. We know this because those are the wrappers we find most often.

Most guidebooks in the past have heavily criticized Tanzania and East Africans for the trash on Kilimanjaro. This makes no sense to me. They never seem to accept that the guidebooks and visitors are the people most responsible for this problem. What we need is for guidebooks and travelers to recognize this and to climb responsibly, cleaning up after themselves. I am hopeful that future travelers will respect Kilimanjaro and our country when they come. Just like when you were a kid, don't expect your mother to clean up after you!

Unfortunately, we also find a lot of disposable hand warmers and toe warmers along the trail. People use them and simply throw them on the ground or even onto the summit. People get very cold at night, and we understand that. But if you bring any of these items with you, pack them and take them down with you. This can help protect the planet. It's the only one we have.

You'll see Coca-Cola and beer for sale at various places when you come down from the mountain and leave the park. We used to have a big business in which people brought bottles of Coca-Cola and beer up to the second camps and sold it to the climbers. That has been stopped, because it resulted in too much trash being left on the mountain. A related problem was that some guides, who were selling drinks as a side business, were not spending enough time taking care of their clients. That's part of why this business was ended. It is not good for guides to become distracted in their jobs.

Overall, the Park Service is doing a good job of cleaning up Kilimanjaro. They require guides to pack and weigh all the trash we collect and take down from the trip, to prove that we're packing trash out that we created while serving clients. The policy now is trash-in, trash-out. This is really helping keep the mountain cleaner for our guests and travelers, a big improvement from the past. You can help: if you find something on the trail, please pick it up and carry it out, or give it to a guide. There is no reason for there to be trash on Kilimanjaro.

When the American guides came over from Montana to teach mountain medicine and safety classes, they talked about a term they use in America: "leave no trace." This is a good concept, and we embrace it in Tanzania and on Kilimanjaro. About half the people who work on getting trash off Kilimanjaro are private employees, and about half work for the Park Service. This has become an extremely important part of Park Service operations. Everyone who works in keeping the mountain clean has to take it extremely seriously or they will lose their jobs.

CHAPTER THIRTY-SEVEN

SOUVENIRS OF YOUR TRIP TO TANZANIA

Coming down off of Kilimanjaro near Mweka Gate.

There are many things you might like to bring home from Tanzania. One very popular item is tanzanite, a rare and precious stone that is endemic to this land. There are carvings of all types of things made from Tanzanian wood; carvings of the animals of East Africa are particularly popular. You can even buy spears, masks and shields, but you will probably need to ship them home. Most airlines won't let you carry spears and knives on airplanes!

Most of the carvings in Tanzania come from the southern part of the country, which is where the best trees for carving grow. Often, village stores will finish the products and polish them before selling them to their clients.

You should bargain on the price for these items because vendors will start very high. Sellers expect you to bargain—it's normal in Tanzania for most products you purchase. It can be fun. Don't let it bother or intimidate you. It's part of our culture. People will actually be disappointed if you *don't* bargain.

You'll usually get a better price if you have a guide from Tanzania with you. This is optional, but if we're with you, we will talk in Swahili and say, "Take care of this person. He is my friend, so take care of him." We also know which stores to avoid, and we'll take you to places that will treat you the best. It's especially helpful to be with a guide when buying tanzanite, because some vendors sell fake pieces, and it's an expensive purchase.

Tanzanite, the trade name for a gem actually called zoisite, was discovered in 1967 in a single location between Arusha and Moshi called Mererlani, near present-day Kilimanjaro International Airport. The Maasai had long known about this brown stone, which turned a brilliant transparent blue after being heated by fires caused by lightening. But the stone was much softer than other gems, like rubies, and they did not consider it to be valuable. There was also no market for it at first, so they ignored it, and only sometimes used it in beading.

Later, the stones were showed by a local prospector to a gem expert named John Saul, and he sent them to his father, Hyman Saul, in New York. Saul gave them to Henry Platt, the vice-president of Tiffany's, who coined the name Tanzanite and declared it to be "the gemstone find of the century." Over the years, tanzanite's value has fluctuated from \$40 to \$1,000 a carat These high-quality gemstones are remarkably beautiful. After being fully heated, they turn a brilliant deep purple—this is what you will see when you buy them.

You can find tanzanite in both Moshi and Arusha. Be sure to get a certificate of documentation, because if it turns out there's something wrong with the stone, you can sue the vendor and get your money back. One of the most popular places to shop is a place called Zebra, at Kibo Tower in Moshi. A large number of tourists have tanzanite on their list as a must-have souvenir from their journey.

There are other types of curios and carvings you can buy if you wish. On the way out if Kilimanjaro National Park, near the public gate, there's a place called the Zebra Mweka store, where you can eat, drink, and shop. It's a big business that is modern, beautiful and safe, and it's probably the largest store in the entire Moshi area.

At this place near Mweka Gate, where many climbers wind up after completing their descent, you'll find a bar with a modern restroom, a business that offers showers, and a spot where you can make your own lunch. There are plenty of tables and chairs and people who will sing for you if you pay them. They do all kinds of Swahili music and they can sing the Kilimanjaro song for you. This is something that you should not miss.

You also might want to buy a very large carving of something like a giraffe. You can find these in many places. I mean really big carvings, like four feet tall or more. You can have them packed in bubble wrap at some of the stores for shipment back home.

In Arusha, you will find many stores with really neat items made here in Tanzania, just like in Moshi. Along the road to

Arusha from Moshi, there are more stores that sell to tourists as well. If you stop in at one, you will have fun just by looking around. You are never required to buy anything. If you're walking around a larger town, expect to be approached by people trying to sell you things. Don't be intimidated. If you're not interested, just tell them politely and they will wander off.

If you do a lot of shopping, think of how you will get things back home and have a plan. There are a couple of good ways to do it. First, if you want to leave items in Tanzania for the guides, porters, and cooks, or if you bring supplies for schools that you plan to leave in Tanzania, this will free up space in your luggage for carvings and other items.

If you are not leaving things behind, then space and weight will be a problem, and you might need to adjust the size of your luggage prior to coming over. Be careful to note the fees for international baggage with your airline so you are not surprised by the cost. Overweight luggage can be exceedingly expensive. Know this information ahead of time and you can always weigh items at your hotel to balance things out. We always have scales here for weighing duffel bags. You can use them to weigh your bags before leaving.

The other way is to just ship things home. Many places will do this for you, but for a price. I would suggest that putting as much as you can in your checked bags is the best way, but if you buy a four-foot-tall giraffe carving, this is something you will likely have to carry on the plane. Most airlines are used to this being done when people return from Africa. Some might accommodate you but not all—and certainly not the discount carriers.

TANZANIAN LIFE AND VILLAGE CULTURE

Driving through village areas on the way to Marangu Gate.

Life in the villages is the heart and soul of Tanzanian culture, and I really hope you can go out and see this for yourself. Walking around a typical village, you'll notice the smells of cooking, the rich vegetation, and the striking red volcanic soil. The rural paths and roads that run around the slopes of Kilimanjaro are truly amazing. People in brightly colored clothes putting out their laundry to dry in the sun under the banana trees, with children playing in the background, is a sight you will not soon forget. During climbing season, the weather will probably be very nice, and the clean mountain air will welcome you. The people you find along the way are also a part of this great experience. This is Tanzania at its best, and I hope you do not miss it. Too many tour operators and guides are all about getting you up and down the mountain. This is of course the main goal, but you need to take the time to see and understand Tanzania life and culture while you're here.

People in the villages know how to enjoy life, family, and friends, and you might learn something from this and take it home with you. There is something about village life that changes your perspective on your own busy life. You can almost hear the ancient drumbeats of our ancestors as you walk around; it is both comforting and deeply moving. It will feel like the land itself is alive with wonder, and that adventure is just around the next bend in the trail.

Most people in the villages are farmers. Every village has a small store, usually in the center, and these combine elements of a farmer's market and a small convenience store, selling a range of manufactured items. To do major shopping, you have to go to a larger place like Moshi.

If you're with a guide and you stop by a village store, you can buy a cold drink or a beer, shop around, and talk to people. It's safe for visitors to stop in villages stores, and it's cheap, much cheaper than shopping in Moshi.

In Tanzania, it's important for people to be clean and have clean clothes. The president of Tanzania has worked hard to make sure that everyone accepts this principle. There's plenty of water in

Tanzania, so it's easy to keep clean. When people go out in public, they wear their best clothes, and you will notice while walking around that people are very nicely dressed. People in Tanzania get a lot of their clothes from the outside world and they take good care of them. Even in the villages, you will see people dressed in brightly colored clothes that are perfectly clean as they wander the dusty trails.

People are religious in my country, primarily practicing a type of either Islam or Christianity. Unlike in many other countries, the relations between Muslims and Christians are very good. We don't see any reason to have differences between them. At Christmastime, Christians will prepare and send food to Muslims, and Muslims will prepare and send food to Christians. We do not understand why Christians and Muslims in other countries do not get along. They come from the same religion and worship the same god. Respecting all faiths is important to Tanzanians.

Many people here also embrace traditional Chagga beliefs. The Chagga system centers on Kilimanjaro, where Ghost is found. People still offer animal to sacrifices on the mountain. This is part of our ancient religion, which predates Christianity and Islam by tens of thousands of years.

A lot of people have TV sets now, and just like anywhere else, they like watching movies, sports, and news. The most popular sport is soccer, and professional basketball is getting more popular all the time. Tanzanians know the names of all the famous players in the NBA and wear T-shirts with their names on them. If you go around in Moshi, you'll find many Chicago Bulls T-shirts: Michael Jordan is still very popular here. People in Tanzania like to play basketball, but we are not very good at it! Only one player from Tanzania has played in the NBA: Hasheem Thabeet.

Action movies are popular in Tanzania. We especially like the movies made in Korea and China, because the filmmakers dub

Climbers from Canada taking a break and visiting
villages around Kilimanjaro. It can be fun!

them using Swahili for us. English movies are also OK for people
who understand them well enough to follow the story.

People in Tanzania love music, and music videos are very popular in local bars! People love R & B and reggae, and a lot of music
made here is influenced by both.

When people get together in their community after dark,
and they have a few drinks, they like to dance traditional dances,
both to Western music and African music. Every tribe has its own
dances, and as the song goes along, the energy level rises, and
people can get pretty crazy!

Old-fashioned home visits are popular here. Especially on
weekends, it's important to go see your relatives and neighbors.
You ask about everything: how is your farm, how are your goats,

how are your cows? People share food, but they especially like to share drinks, including home-made beer.

Many people in Tanzania would like to buy a car, but they're very expensive, so bikes are more commonly used in town. As you get farther up on the slopes of Kilimanjaro, bike use declines because the roads are too steep. People who live along the coast or in central Tanzania use bikes a lot. It's flatter in those areas, especially along the coast of the Indian Ocean.

Even in a village like the one I grew up in, people still want to go to school and even university someday, but it's expensive once you get past primary school. (This part of your education is provided by the government for free.) Only about half of all students will be able to go to secondary school and only about 25 percent will go on to high school. Even less go to university. My kids are aiming for a bachelor's degree, if I can finance it.

In Tanzanian culture, if someone becomes a doctor or lawyer or some type of professional, they will help out the rest of their family. This is an important part of how we live, sharing our resources with everyone else. Because your parents helped you, you must give them something back later. In Chagga culture, fulfilling this bargain is seen as very important. People believe that if you do not do this, something bad will happen to you. Even in our place names, you will see some of this reflected: for example, we re-named the top of Mount Meru and we now call it Socialist Peak. We all do things together and take care of others.

When you are in Tanzania, some people may invite you to visit their home. Generally, tour operators discourage this, in part because they're concerned that Tanzanians might give their visitors alcohol or food that isn't properly cooked and would make them sick. If you're invited into a home, you should ask your local guide to help your hosts understand these concerns.

Most people in Tanzania live with their extended families, including their parents, kids, and grandkids. Traditional beehive huts, made of mud, are almost gone these days. Most Tanzanians now live in modern houses built using cement, and they usually have running water and electricity. These big changes are fairly recent, happening only in the last ten years or so. My more modern house is not yet complete.

I used to keep cattle, but the area where I live now, outside of Moshi, is becoming less isolated as the cities expand. You also have to pay a tax if you have goats and cattle, which became a real problem for me, so I don't have them anymore. I have chickens, and I get eggs from them every day. I used to have four cows, but one died, I sold two, and I gave the last one to my uncle.

Someday when I retire and go back into farming, I will move to a more rural area, because there is not enough room for a real farm where I live now. I will not raise cows in the future, just goats and pigs. Pigs are a very good business in Tanzania. If you raise them, you can sell them in six months to a year.

Another thing changing the farming business is the use of cell phones. With a mobile application like WhatsApp, you can post a picture of your goats or your bananas for people to purchase. You can even negotiate the price through the phone. This is a huge change in how the marketplace works in Tanzania. Technology is reaching into the most remote places in our culture, and some of it good and some of it bad.

People who live in our villages are generally happy, but they don't make a lot of money. Income often depends on the time of the year and the weather. When there are strong rains, then there are more crops, so business is much better in the fall, thanks to the increased farming production.

When younger people make enough money, they will often save up and buy a motorcycle. The ones they buy are made in

China and are fairly inexpensive. A motorcycle allows young people to drive down into villages from farms and visit with their friends and family. You can drive them on very narrow trails, which you can't do with a car.

If young people in Tanzania meet and like each other, and they want to get married, they *can* do this on their own. But if they do it that way, the marriage may not be blessed. To get married properly, each person must go to the other person's family and talk with them, to make sure that the proposed union is OK with everyone. This shows respect to the families and elders. If people get married without the blessings of both families, then they can expect that something bad will happen in the future. Most boys are at least 20 before they get married. Most girls are around 16.

If older people make and save enough money, an important purchase for them is an automobile, which they can use to go to town, to a market, or to church. Most everyone goes to church on Sunday. Sometimes they'll do fellowship during the week, but the majority still believe it's good to go on Sunday. Young people still go to church, but not quite as much as the older people do today.

After church, people like to have barbecue and get together and visit. The men will head to a local bar for barbecue; the women go to their homes and prepare a big meal. Families will often hold either a big lunch or a big dinner, with numerous guests.

If you're visiting Tanzania and you're here on a Sunday, you would be welcome to attend any type of local church or mosque. They might even announce you as a visitor and have you stand up. You would also be welcome to go to a bar after church. (Again, I would again recommend that visitors do not eat the barbecue.) Church may not exactly resemble what you're imagining from a Western perspective. Although it will be faith-based, it is also a cultural meeting place for our local communities. Tanzanians are very social and love to get together and visit, sing, eat, and dance.

Many Tanzanians are in the tourist and travel industry, so visitors are a regular part of their lives. Even people who live on the farms know how important tourism is to our economy. They are fine with this and welcome the business. There is a universal language among all humans that touches on warmth, friendship, and inclusiveness. Nowhere is this truer than in Tanzania.

Among the annual celebrations that come up, New Year's is a big holiday in Tanzanian cities—for all tribes, but especially the Chagga. People come down from the villages and Moshi gets very crowded. New Year's is an important family holiday. Extended families get together, often returning to Moshi from far away, and they talk about the previous year and their plans for the next. We also pray to God or Ghost at this time. Muslims and Christians are friends, so they will celebrate together even if they don't share the same holidays and beliefs.

There is peace in Tanzania, and a spirit of charity. Even if you don't have food, people will share it with you. People can live without a lot of money and be happy if they have fresh food. No one who walks into a bar will not be served a beer, even if they do not have money.

Bananas are very popular in Tanzania, but especially so on the slopes of Kilimanjaro. These bananas are very sweet. In the old days, people used to pick wild bananas from the forest, but today most bananas are grown by farmers. A nice thing about bananas is that they are safe for tourists because you peel them. The fruit inside is always safe. How can a person not be happy if they can grow or harvest their own food locally?

This is a little of what life is like in Tanzania. I really hope you will come to a village and get to meet the people. They will welcome you warmly and it would be a shame to come so far and not get to know the people who live in more rural areas. This is the heart of Tanzania, in the shadow of Kilimanjaro. This is the real Africa, my home.

CHAPTER THIRTY-NINE

LOCAL TRIBAL SYSTEMS & GOVERNMENT

Classic view of Zebra Rocks on the Marangu Route.

The Old Ways

As we have discussed, some guidebooks in the past have been dismissive and disrespectful when talking about Tanzania and our government. This is unfortunate. All countries have their own systems and challenges. We are no different. Some writers have used Western cultural and religious standards when writing about Tanzania. They thought that they were somehow superior and had all the knowledge and answers.

A couple of the most prominent guidebooks on the market today for Kilimanjaro actually use the word "savages" when describing the people of East Africa, and say that our people needed to be "civilized" by missionaries, colonists, and explorers during that era. In my view, the opposite was actually true.

This is the same old thinking from colonial times, and it is no less wrong now than it was then. Looking at the world-wide political landscape in 2021, some writers from other countries might want to rethink their insensitive and incorrect assumptions about Tanzania. Terrible things have been said about African countries by Western leaders. One was said by an American president who I won't quote here. This man is no longer in office, so I think you know who I mean. I will not honor his name by writing it here. How can a leader say something like that about our great land and the warm and welcoming people here in Africa?

Tanzania is a free country in which we govern ourselves by our own systems and ways, and we do a great job of educating our young people. We are a happy and peaceful land, welcoming to outsiders. How many countries today can say the same?

Tanzanians are remarkably united. I am very proud to be from here. I am also proud of our many tribes that live together in peace and appreciate our cultural differences. My family and friends in the villages feel the same. We may not be the richest people in the world, but we are living in peace, harmony, and happiness. The fact that the quality of life is good should be the measure of any independent self-governed country.

What I hope is that we can turn the page on how people think and write about Africa. Let's stop using the old colonial stereotypes that depicted Africa as a dark and unenlightened place. We should use the proper historical and local names of places that honor this land and our ancestors, and remove guidebook references to colonialists who came to steal, pillage, and rape our people, culture, and lands. I am optimistic that this book will be the beginning of such efforts. My children and grandchildren should see and read the true history of Tanzania, not the colonial version. Let us move forward with a suitable new history and understanding of Tanzanian culture, government, and religion.

A New Way of Thinking About East Africa

There are at least 121 tribes in Tanzania, and there are smaller tribes not included in this count. More than 90 percent of Tanzanians speak Swahili. We can usually tell what area or tribe people are from by their local accent.

There are four main Chagga tribes: the Uru, Machame, Marangu, and Rombo. They are spread around the slopes of Kilimanjaro. Each has its own chief, but the top chief over everyone comes from the Marangu.

Chiefdoms are hereditary, handed down through families. Traditionally, the chief had control over all the lands, and he would allocate land to the people of the tribe. He would also control all the rules and the punishments for the tribe when this was needed, although people usually got along just fine in their own local communities. In our time, some elements of this system have faded out. After Tanzania gained its independence in December 1961, things have of course changed to some degree.

We still respect the chief, even though he no longer has as much real power as in the past. As you know, we believe on Ghost, and the chief leads the animal sacrifice and praying directed to this deity. Most Chagga people still respect the chief, but younger people are not following this tradition as closely. Still, the role of the chief remains an important part of each community in modern, post-independence Tanzania.

Elders and leaders in the villages and towns work under these four tribes. Although a village will have a leader much like anywhere else, there are also elected officials from everywhere in Tanzania. The officials in all the different areas represent the people to the national representative government, or what you might think of as our parliament. The clan leaders locally deal with internal issues within the tribe and they still have quite a bit of power. The majority of this power goes to the clan leader. The elected official for that area—who represents the group to the government in Dodama—still has to go back to the clan leader and consult with them. The clan leaders are deeply respected among the local people, but they are not dictators.

This is the one major misconception about historical governing in East Africa, and it also finds its roots in the colonial era. Westerners and Europeans could not understand the concept of collective local governance. They could only understand the concept of a king, dictator, or powerful leader who had total control over everyone and ruled with threats of violence and strict laws. In our culture, we usually solve most of our problems collectively on a local level. People talk and come to consensus with solutions that make sense to everyone. We are accountable to each other, so everyone works together to do the right thing for the community. Outsiders could not understand this concept, and they still do not today.

In our system, people pay taxes to the national government, including a tax on cell phone airtime, income tax, car parking, and other things. The income tax—one part of the old British system that we've kept—is around 18 percent. If you make $200, the government will take $36 in value-added tax from your income. It is quite a bit, but not that different from most other countries, or maybe even less.

Farmers also have to pay taxes when their crops go to market, so it's not just the tourism industry that funds government services around Kilimanjaro. When you go to the market, they give you a small space where you can sell your crops. You have to pay for the table, and then they give you a receipt for the day. The government sets up the markets and then they contract with a private company that rents space out to the vendors and farmers. the tax is paid back to the government from the vendor. Like everywhere else in the world, people generally feel that their tax rates are a little too high. Businesspeople and farmers both say the same thing, but infrastructure, hospitals, and schools are all paid for with taxes. Good things come from the taxes people pay.

National Service and Independence Day

Every ninth of December, we have a big Independence Day celebration throughout Tanzania, an important occasion that marks the end of British rule in 1961. People like to go to the big towns and watch sporting events. There are parades and songs. Many people stay in the villages on Independence Day, but they like getting together in bars and homes for beer and barbecue. The government puts on parades using soldiers from the army.

A few people join the Army, but we also have what we call a national service that is mandatory for people who finish high school. If you find that you like the service, after six months you can then join the Army. If you don't like it, you just go back to your job and old life.

I was in national service for one year. I went when I was younger. It's really tough. They teach you how to use weapons, how to fight, and how to protect our national security. I did my service in Dodoma.

We don't pay anyone for their time in the National Service. You stay in a camp in tents and they feed you. Like I said, it's difficult. Women have to go into National Service as well, but mostly it's for men. It's our responsibility to serve our country and defend against the enemies of Tanzania.

That is just a little bit more about Tanzania, our government and our people, so you can understand it better when you come to visit and to be our welcomed guest!

CHAPTER FORTY

THE MAASAI

There are many tribes in Tanzania, all with their own cultures and customs and sometimes even their own local languages. Most speak Swahili, except for the Maasai tribe.

The Maasai are an amazing people. They used to come from just the central dry regions of Tanzania and Kenya, but you can find them virtually everywhere in Tanzania today. They move with the weather and they travel to where their cattle can graze.

Maasai sometimes come to Moshi and Arusha. They drink beer and they can go into a local bar. They also really like barbecue, but it's difficult to share barbecue with them because when they make it, it's still very raw inside. Most people in my tribe don't like their meat as red as the Maasai do.

The Maasai live in the wild, tending to their cattle, and they carry a spear and a large knife—two or three feet long—in case they get into a confrontation with a wild animal and have to kill it. They are very brave. I like to see the Maasai and I enjoy watching them when they come into the villages.

In a village, the Maasai will take their spear into a bar, even into a police station. The government will let them do this. No other tribes or people are allowed to walk around town with weapons except the Maasai. The police know that the Maasai are

Maasai at Oldavai Gorge with spears for sale.

used to living in the bush, so they're not frightened of them when they bring a spear or large knife into town. They police rarely have trouble with the Maasai.

Before people came to understand the Maasai, they usually feared them, because they are very fierce-looking, and they always have their weapons in their hands. The first time I saw them, I was with a group of my friends and somebody said, "Oh, this is not good. These people have a big knife, so take care." Nowadays, people know the Maasai better and they are not as afraid of them as they used to be.

Sometimes the Maasai will steal cows from another person in Tanzania. That's the big problem with the Maasai, and though it's not quite as bad as it was, it's still a problem. The Maasai believe they own all cattle in the world, so if they find one, it just means the cows are returning to their rightful owners when they take them back. The government now has a policy of fining them and taking them to a police station if they're caught stealing other people's cows. The Maasai do not want to get locked up. If they are taken to the police, they will be honest and say, "Yes, I stole the cow." They never want to be put in jail. They are deeply frightened of this concept: a jail with bars and a lock, a place where, once you're inside, you cannot leave. They do not understand it. They can just give up and die. Police know this and they are careful about this cultural difference.

You should never take a picture of the Maasai before asking permission. This could be dangerous. If you ask them first, they might say it is OK, but they might also ask you to pay them.

I sometimes run into Maasai in the forest. When you talk to them, they often ask for water. They really like water because they generally stay in very dry areas. If you go to Maasai country, you should take extra water, because they will want you to share it with them.

Young Maasai posing for a picture. These guys wanted $5 for the shot.

The Maasai speak their own language. I do not understand it and most people I know don't understand it, either. We usually can only get through their basic greetings and that's about it.

The Maasai can be very friendly, but you never want to provoke them, because if you do, they may cut you with a knife. If you want to talk to them, you have to go down and greet them first, then tell them what you want to do. Maybe you want to take a picture, but you have to talk about it first. You can say, "I want to go to your *boma*, to your village." They have to go back to the village and discuss it first. Then they will come back and talk to you.

If they come back and the village has talked about it, you might get permission and can go to the village. You will be very welcome, but you will probably have to pay something. If you go, you will see one of the last remaining wild tribes in Africa, who still live much as they have for tens of thousands of years.

You will also see the Maasai, in small groups, just wandering around in many locations, often in the national parks or on the side of a road somewhere. If they stop, you might talk to them. This is different from visiting one of their villages.

With the money they receive, the Maasai will send someone from the family every week or month to the city, like Moshi or Arusha. Everybody in the family of the village has to say, "I want this and this and this," and then someone has to collect all this information for everything that everyone wants from the town. This one person has the list of the things for everyone—an entire family or maybe even five families.

The Maasai men used to always wear red, or what we call the Maasai blanket. But things change, and today the Maasai like to wear short cargo pants underneath their blanket, because they like having a lot of pockets to put things in, like tobacco, money, and other items. Sometimes women can wear blue, black, or white, but generally the men like a blanket with red on it.

When you are in Tanzania, I really hope you get to see the Maasai. They have not gone far from their ancient traditional ways, even today. They are a regal people who are very proud. Their kids do not go to school much, but some are starting to do so. They like to tend to their cows in the bush and that is their main job. They can be very fierce in defending their cattle from wild animals, even the lion or the leopard. Can you imagine killing a lion or a leopard with a spear? The Maasai can do this. They are very brave. If you want to visit one of their villages, please talk to a guide first and make sure you do it properly. Be safe and culturally responsible, but in any event, do not just drive up to their village and go in uninvited. That would be very dangerous.

CHAPTER FORTY-ONE

SAFARI!

This is Amrod Olotu from Wildersun Safari with my friends in the Serengeti.

Now that you've come this far with me, I need you to consider one last thing to make your journey the adventure of a lifetime. It is Safari! You should not come to African and learn so much without continuing your journey and seeing other Tanzanian National

Parks. Kilimanjaro is only a small part of what this country has to offer.

I will tell you a secret that most books don't include: many people who both climb Kilimanjaro and go see one, two, or three other national parks on safari are surprised by what becomes their favorite part of the trips. Many who really wanted to climb the mountain find out that they like the parks and wildlife better than the climb. Many who came to see the parks and climb Kilimanjaro reach the opposite conclusion. This is very common. You never know which adventure you will like best in the end.

Among our great national parks are Serengeti, Ngorongoro, Tarangire, and Lake Manyara, and I would strongly suggest that you see at least three of them when you visit, spending three or four days on safari if you can. I would also suggest that you talk to your hotel or tour operator and set this up ahead of time, as a package. Moshi is the center of the climbing business, but most hotels there can also book a safari for you. Likewise, businesses in Arusha, which tend to book more safaris, can also book Kilimanjaro climbs, even though this is not their main focus. In Moshi, we don't get a lot of people who come here only to do a safari. That is more common in Arusha.

If you are booking through an international guiding service, they will almost certainly offer a safari as part of the package with your climb of Kilimanjaro, or you can do the climb as a trip by itself. Please do not fail to take advantage of a safari, though. If you want to book your safari separately, or even book it once you are here, you can do that, but the companies get filled up, and it will definitely cost more to do it this way.

Prices for safari usually include transportation, hotels, food, touring vehicles, and guides, all as part of one package. Accommodations vary: you can stay in anything from a tent to a first-class hotel. Different people like different levels of service, and you'll find that a hotel or guiding service that offers, say, higher-end safaris may also offer similar levels of service on Kilimanjaro. This can take some of the guesswork out if it. Hotels and quality guide services really care about their reputations, and they don't want you to have a bad experience to tell others about back home.

Researching safaris takes us back to the internet, so I'll caution you again about trusting everything you see and read there. You should never give anyone money until you are sure you have checked them out properly. If you're booking through a reputable international guide service from your home country, you won't have much to worry about.

Some people come to Tanzania only to go on safari, and have no interest in climbing Kilimanjaro. Travelers who do this usually go to Arusha from the start, rather than Moshi, the climbing hub. This is because many of the flights to the Serengeti leave from Arusha Airport. Quite a few people fly out to begin their safari, and then drive by the many national parks on the way back. This is a good way to do it, but you can drive both ways if you wish.

When you book both your trip and climb together, you'll often do a safari with a specific company that is already part of that company's overall program. If you do it this way, you will not have a lot of options, but there are still some things to think over in terms of the choices you'll be given. For example, you do not need to go with people you don't know if you want to spend a bit more for a private vehicle, or even devise your own itinerary, as opposed to a pre-set one that can't be changed. You could even come and book without a specific itinerary at all and just make it up as you go, but this will cost more.

Not all that long ago, there weren't many safari companies. Today there are hundreds. Many provide outstanding experiences, but as with anything else, you need to do research. If your trip is booked through a reputable hotel in Moshi, or with a company in

You do not want to fall into a Hippo pool!

your home country—such as International Mountain Guides or Rainier Mountaineering—you will probably not be disappointed. They can take all of the guesswork out of it. And I'll mention again that I am using these companies as examples—I have no business relationship with them, and they have not paid me to say their names. There are many good companies out there. There are also many reputable hotels in Tanzania that can book your safari and your climb. Some are experts at this and take the time to learn what you are looking for, as opposed to pushing you into something that just makes them money.

The hotel you'll stay in while on the safari will likely be part of the package. The lodgings usually include meals but not alcoholic drinks. All your transportation will be part of your safari, including in-country flights if they're necessary.

Most of the vehicles that companies use for safari are fairly consistent—that is, they look like what you would think a safari vehicle should look like, with four-wheel-drive, high-clearance, and body and window designs that make it easy to get clear views of wildlife. The tops often pop up so you can stand and take photographs. Range Rovers and Toyota Land Cruisers are common. Some are a bit larger than others—including ones with open sides and variations of the pop-up tops—and you can rent a private vehicle if you want one.

This is something to think about. It doesn't cost much more to book your own safari vehicle, and if you do, you'll have complete control over where you go each day. This way of doing it can provide greater flexibility than safaris where the route is set out ahead of time and doesn't change much. In a safari with a fixed route, you'll also be in the vehicle with people you don't know. Not everyone may have your likes and dislikes. For these and other reasons, a private vehicle may be worth the extra cost.

You can book a budget safari for as little as $150 a night, with everything included, but I wouldn't recommend this for most people, because it's going to be rustic and probably not very comfortable. The mid-range is roughly $350 a night per person. These are very good! Luxury accommodations usually cost around $750 a night and these are amazing—with very personal service at every turn, among other things. High-end safari, with everything included, can cost more than $1,500 a night per person. These defy description, and they offer everything you could possibly imagine in terms of service and quality. How can someone spend this type of money on safari? Well, if you have the budget, anything is possible, maybe for a movie star or professional sports player? I don't know how someone could afford this myself, but they can.

The internet can be helpful during your search, because you can see photos of the vehicles your company uses and the hotel

Here are two Cheetah brothers. They are beautiful creatures.

you'll be in. You can also fact-check these images—which, after all, are advertisements—by comparing them to photos taken by people who have booked with these companies. What you see there is an accurate depiction of what you'll get. While you're looking, search for people who share your expectations and style and see what worked for them. If you select a company that looks good, ask for local references in the area where you live. Tens of thousands of people have done this prior to you. Paying close attention to personal references is the best way to make a smart choice.

In general, I'm not going to recommend any one company over another—too many of you have different preferences for that approach to make sense—but I will mention one company as an example, and just for fun.

It's one of the oldest: Wildersun Safari, which is based in Arusha. I mention them because of a man named Amrod Olotu, one of the most experienced safari drivers in Tanzanian history. He got started as a driver over four decades ago, at a time when there were only about five companies in this business, and over the years he's earned a sterling reputation because of his knowledge, skill, and attention to detail.

Amrod took my friends Christopher and April Hurst out on safari a couple of times, the last one in 2009. They asked me to mention him and to share how much fun it was for them to go out alone with him. One morning, they woke up and had breakfast and talked to Olotu about their plans for the day. He said he could take them to see a place very few visitors ever visit. They agreed, and he took them deep into the wilderness, into the middle of the great migration that occurs from the Serengeti to the Masai Mara in Kenya. Every year, between July and early October, great numbers of animals go on this migration, all at the same time.

Christopher and April told me they saw literally millions of animals; they said there were no words for what they had experienced. The day was long and rough, most of it cross-country and not on roads at all. They saw all these animals in their natural environment and saw virtually no one else during the entire day. That can give you an idea of how remote and wild a day on safari can actually be. You would need a highly experienced guide for such a trip.

Which National Parks should you visit? Most tours will take you to several. Probably the most famous and popular is Serengeti, which sits near the northern border of Tanzania with Kenya, between Lake Victoria to the west and Kilimanjaro to the east. Ngorongoro Crater is also very popular, and it has some of the best hotels anywhere in Tanzania. My favorite is the Ngorongoro Serena Safari Lodge, but you can't go wrong with most of the

Saddle-billed Stork in the Serengeti National Park.

hotels in this area. The elevation at the top of the crater rim is 7,500 feet (2,300 meters), so it's going to get pretty cold up there at night, but the days are usually very warm and sunny. Many hotels keep their outside lights dim at night so you can see the night sky. They will be pointed down onto the trails and pathways around the hotel property for safety. A few elephants also frequent the crater rim, but they will not bother you.

The crater here was once a mountain much larger than Kilimanjaro. It blew up and collapsed a very long time ago. Inside it, you will find many amazing birds and animals, but it is probably most famous for the rhinoceros that live there. They are often hard to find around Africa, but they live in this place, and of course people want to see them. They almost seem prehistoric, like a creature from the distant time of the dinosaurs. The crater rim is deep and steep, but at the bottom there is a huge area of grassland populated by a large number of wild animals. In the grasses you will also see many small animals, including different types of wild cats.

You should also stop by Olduvai Gorge on the way. Many tours of the national parks will include this. It is on the road from Ngorongoro Crater to Serengeti. The oldest records of all human habitation and tools on earth have been found here. There is a museum where you can learn about our ancient, shared ancestors. Visiting the Olduvai Gorge feels like a deeply religious experience to many people. On some days, the Maasai will be here with items to sell and to greet visitors. There are no meals available, but you can go on a one-to-two-hour guided tour, or just visit the interpretative center on your own.

On safari, you will see things you had never even imagined. Even when flying from Arusha to the landing strip in the Serengeti, your pilot will have to make a pass over the runway to make sure elephants are not in the way. I am not joking about this! It is truly a wonder to see these lands in the parks. There is no other place like them in the world. When you land and are on your way to your hotel for the first night, you may see cape buffaloes, giraffe, elephants, hyena, and warthogs—just along this route. You will want to see everything and stop to take pictures, but there will be so much more in the days to come.

How long should you spend on safari? People usually do three or four nights. You can certainly do more, but I think you'll find that, after four days on safari, and having done your climb prior to that, you will be very well satisfied. (Some people spend longer on safari, but these are usually people who came to Africa for that alone and did not climb Kilimanjaro.) Also remember that you may want to spend an extra day or two visiting a village or some other activity, so make sure you factor in enough time for everything you hope to do. Your climb and safari will be excellent, but they won't allow you much interaction with people and communities in Tanzania. This is especially true on safaris—they mainly happen in national parks, and not many people live there.

The hotels in the Tanzanian National Parks are very nice. Some use traditional African designs, and you might even sleep in a hut-like room that from the outside looks like the traditional beehive hut I grew up in. Of course, you will not find cattle or goats inside to keep you warm at night! The furnishings inside are modern, and you'll find everything you need for your comfort after a long day outside. Some hotels have local artists and craft items on display for sale. Many have a gift shop. Evening entertainment may also be available at some locations. It can be a lot of fun to see Tanzanian singing and dancing groups.

At night, there is excellent food service with numerous options. Many of the hotels have a bar, where you can relax with a drink and meet other travelers. I like to say that it is very lazy to be on safari after climbing Kilimanjaro. This is a good thing. You have earned it!

When having a drink, as always, be careful. These places do an excellent job in preparing safe food, but microbes can find their way into your body in unexpected ways—for example, in the water used to make ice. I'd either have the bartender leave the ice out or consider another drink entirely. Remember that we have a lot of really great beers in Tanzania. Try them!

There are two drinks you should be very cautious about. One is a local distilled product called Konyagi, a spirit made from sugar cane. It is popular, but it is not for everyone, and some travelers have described some interesting experiences after drinking it, if you take my meaning. True or not, some travelers say they have visions and unusual dreams. The second drink is our local banana beer. *Do not drink this*—it is not for you. It is always available in

The Warthog is always watching to see that a lion will not come
and eat them. They have to get on their knees to eat.

villages, but travelers should not drink it because of how we make
it and the food-handling methods that are used. Our real beers
are excellent, so stick to them. If you fail to follow my suggestions,
you were warned.

For breakfast, you might have an omelet at the breakfast bar,
and almost all hotels and operators will provide you with a box
lunch for the day. Some companies will offer full gourmet meals
when you stop for lunch—it all depends on what package you
purchase.

At night on safari, if you chose to wake up and wander around
and see the stars, remember that you are in a very wild part of
Africa now. This is where the animals live and most come out to
hunt in the dark. Be very cautious and make sure you know where

it is safe to walk around. Talk to your guides and hotel workers to ensure that you don't have an unplanned, up-close encounter with an elephant or lion.

The first time I went on safari, I had to sleep in a tent and there were animals all around at night. They were making a lot of noise. I was not used to it, and it was a little scary to me at first. On a more positive note, I enjoyed how easy it was to be with clients and not have to climb the mountain each day. It was fun to be lazy! Then one day I got scared again, because a baboon got on top of our vehicle, and after a while he came inside! I did not like this too much, but such things can happen on safari. This is all part of the adventure.

This brings us to daytime encounters with animals. You will be amazed by how close you get to them, even lions, elephants, and cheetahs. Don't worry: your guide knows how to keep you safe, but at first you'll very likely wonder how you can be safe at such close distances. The truth is, the animals don't care much about you, and most of the time they will not even look in your direction. They are not hunting humans. They are only interested in animals that they want to eat. They know the difference.

For instance, cheetahs only eat a very small range of animals that they can catch and kill. They are remarkably fast, and you might see them hunting, but they can't kill a large animal and they will not try. A lion will not spend the energy to kill a small animal that doesn't feed the pride—a group of lions—so catching smaller animals is not worth it. Lions will stalk and eat a zebra, buffalo, or wildebeest, because it is worth the effort. They do not want to eat you. Maybe we do not taste good to them, I do not know for sure.

You will likely see a pride of lions, and you may notice that the female lions do most of the hunting. You also might see a group of young lions under a tree all together. This is where their mothers leave them when they are out hunting. Where are the fathers?

They will almost always be sleeping. That is what they do most of the day. In fact, you will find that they are very lazy and sleep about 20 hours a day. It is unlikely you will even see them awake. You may see lions from very close range, and often you will come across a group of lions with a fresh kill, maybe even on the dirt road when you are driving by. The lions will usually be sleeping after they eat.

Out on the grassy plains, you will feel the wind blowing and see animals all around. The sun is hot, and you will welcome any breezes. Watch carefully around the edges of groups of Thomson's gazelles and see if there are cheetahs stalking them from the grasses. Something is always happening. You will see warthogs kneeling on their front legs, eating while watching to see if an animal will come to eat them. Groups of buffaloes will be near the scrubby trees, and they will always look angry and irritated.

Throughout the plains of Africa, you will see the zebra. (The name is pronounced zebra, not zeeebra. Zeb, like Deb, but with a Z. People from Europe and America pronounce the name wrong, for some reason.) They are very fast, and lions like to eat them. You can tell the males from the females because of their markings. The males are black with white stripes and the females are white with black stripes.

Hippopotamus will be bathing in pools, with the water supporting their huge weight and keeping them cool. It is not common to see them out of the water, and they can be very dangerous and ill-tempered if they are. They are actually quite fast over short distances, and they have powerful jaws. You might believe that a lion or leopard is the most dangerous animal, but this is not true. I can tell you that the hippopotamus is the most dangerous of all large wild animals and that about 500 people a year are killed by them in Africa. Your guides will know how to find them in places where you can see them safely and get good pictures. Interestingly,

Zebras can be chased and caught by the lions for a meal sometimes.

hippos cannot swim at all and they sink to the bottom of the pond or a river and they walk on the bottom or hop to the surface to breath. If the water is too deep, they can drown. They only look like they are swimming.

Leopards are often very difficult to see, and if you do see one, it will probably be up in a tree during the day, sleeping. They might have their kill from the night before up with them on a branch. Leopards are very powerful climbers.

While you're looking up in the trees, you might see some remarkably large snakes up there. They are huge—some can even kill an antelope and devour it whole! The largest snake in Tanzania is the Serengeti rock python, which can grow up to 20 feet long. They eat monkeys and can even catch and eat a gazelle. Other snakes found in the parks include the green mamba, the Egyptian

Leopards will usually be seen in trees during the day.

cobra, and puff adders. The adders usually move slowly, but when they attack, they are one of the fastest snakes in Africa. They are very common in all Tanzanian National Parks. They have venom and can harm a person. You should not approach them.

You will certainly see many elephants. They are wonderful and amazing creatures that are a lot of fun to observe. You will want to stop and watch what they are doing. Elephants are very smart, have different personalities, and usually really do have great memories: they can remember people they have met from many years ago. Their family structures are very strong, and they have deep feelings for each other. I really hope you learn a lot more about them, and you will feel different after spending some time in their homelands.

As you ride along on safari, you will feel a sense of wonder about the amazing varieties of birds. There are different types of birds everywhere you go, and their numbers and beauty will surprise you. You might see a grey- crowned crane, our national bird, or a saddle-billed stork, two of my favorites. Our largest bird is of course the ostrich, which does not fly but is very fast and powerful. Two of the larger flying birds are the secretary bird, a long-legged bird of prey, and the kori bustard, a big, ground-dwelling bird that eats many things, like snakes.

Monkeys are found in many areas, usually close to water, trees, or lakes. Species like blue monkeys and colobus are very common, and you will probably see baboons in large family groups as well. They often will walk across the roads in large numbers, and you will have to wait for them to pass. They are not friendly to people and you don't want to provoke them or make fun of them.

I know we already talked about the Maasai in a previous chapter, but you could possibly be out in the middle of what seems like nowhere in a national park, and then along will come a line of most regal looking people in very traditional wear, with spears, and they will be trotting along at a steady pace. They will be the Maasai. You will see the distinctive red or purple clothing and they will not even likely look at you at all. I do not know what they are doing. You will not know what they are doing or where they are going either. They are just going somewhere. Even if you were just sitting there and you saw them off in the distance, they could come by and then go off past you and never even look your way as they pass. They look very fierce and confident. This happens in national park areas and this is where they can be seen in their normal historic areas.

Most trips will also involve a stop at a park with a lake or a large wetland area, because these places are attractive to birds and animals of all types. Unless you stay in Africa for a couple of months, you will not be able to see all the Tanzanian National Parks. We have 22 of them, and 15 percent of our country has

Kind and friendly, there are many elephants in East Africa today.

been set aside for parks and conservation areas. Even with a whole year to spend, you would not even begin to see everything that the Tanzanian National Parks have to offer our visitors. They are vast.

Overall, it is very difficult for me to say which safari would be best for you. You can't go wrong, because there is so much to see, and it really depends on personal taste. I would say that if your preference is to see animals—and not a lot of other people—you may wish to book a private safari, with a highly experienced guide who can take you off the beaten path. Plan for a bumpy, long, and dusty day if you do this, but for your efforts, you will be richly rewarded. Most people will be more than happy with a conventional safari. You will have plenty of opportunities to take pictures and your guides will be experts at pointing out and describing

Cape Buffaloes can be bad-tempered, and you do not want to provoke them.

creatures and their habits. You will see many animals no matter where you go in Tanzania's national parks.

You will probably end your safari by deciding that you have a favorite animal. I will share mine with you: it is the giraffe. They are graceful and beautiful. They usually move slowly and in a sort of rhythm, but they can also run very fast if they wish to. They are the tallest animals on earth, but they can run at 35 miles per hour over short distances. They are well-suited for the wild plains and only need to drink water once every few days. They live most of their lives standing and can even sleep while standing up. They only need 30 minutes of sleep a day! These beautiful creatures were hunted to near-extinction by Europeans and Westerners, but we are trying to better protect them so they will be here for future generations to see.

During the times when European and Western colonial powers and missionaries invaded Africa, white hunters came from around the world to kill these amazing and regal animals, often just to watch them die or take trophies. When Tanzania became an independent country, we chose, as a people and a nation, to protect these and other wild animals from such a terrible fate. We decided that our future, and our country, should be about protecting natural resources and wild places. In the long run, it is much better to have people come see and photograph these amazing animals rather than slaughter them for the fun of it.

On safari, you might take time to think about how Africa and our local cultures and people have been criticized in old guidebooks, movies, and literature. If we were still in the colonial period and not a free and independent nation, it is highly unlikely that there would be a single large animal left alive. Much of our

The Wildebeest are everywhere in the National Parks and lions can eat them.

language and customs would be long dead if the invaders had completed what they set out to do in Africa.

Today, we are also suffering from the effects of climate change. In Africa, we understand the land, nature, and the very rhythm of life. You will feel it here like no other place in the world, and you will see nature as it once was. But we must all strive to save this very special place. Climate change is a world-wide problem that affects us all, especially in the natural environments of East Africa.

When you come to visit the parks, you too will become part of the process of protecting these wild creatures and lands. The funds that keep the ecotourism system in place come from visitors like you. Since we gained our independence, we have tried to protect these lands and animals, because we believe our future and the future of the natural world are tied together.

We are committed to keeping and expanding our wild places. We are happy to be rid of the wasteful and foolish practices of the colonial period. Here in Africa, we have a better and more civilized way for you to come and experience the wonders of nature. This is how it should be. This is how it always should have been. This is Tanzania, and you are most welcome to come and be our guest!

CHAPTER FORTY-TWO

FLYING BACK TO EAST AFRICA

See, I am driving back to Africa! Just kidding, I took a plane.

Now my book is almost done. I hope you have learned everything you need to know to have a safe and successful trip to Tanzania, and to do your climb of Kilimanjaro. If you have read everything

Here I am at Rainier Mountaineering and Whittaker Basecamp near Mt Rainier
in Washington State. It's a cool place. I will never forget my trip to America.

and prepared properly, you are ready. I may see you when you are
here. I hope I do.

When my journey to America was coming to a close, I got
to San Francisco and was waiting to board my Boeing 747 on
Virgin Atlantic. I could see it parked at the gate under a dreary
and cloudy sky. There was almost too much to think about, and I
was also thinking of my family and home back in Tanzania. I felt
so many things all at once. America and this great journey had
changed me, and I would never be the same. You may feel something like this when you wait to board the airplane that will take
you home from Africa. I felt happiness and sadness at the same
time. I cannot say.

Once again, I was on my way, with another long journey
through England and then onto another plane to take me home.

I was used to this process now, my fears far in the distance. These were long flights, and I remember looking out the window and seeing the sands of Egypt or Libya, I am not sure which. This seemed like a desolate place to me; I was lost in my thoughts once again.

I eventually landed in Nairobi and took the long, crowded bus ride back to Moshi. I do not know, but I think our journeys may be the same in some ways. I hope that my story has helped me write a book that will have meaning for you when you're here. Good luck!

Oh, and I almost forgot: I was just kidding about the markings on the zebras. They are all the same.

CHAPTER FORTY-THREE

THOUGHTS ON ERICK'S JOURNEY TO AMERICA, BY CHRISTOPHER HURST

I met Erick Kivelege when I was climbing Kilimanjaro for the second time, via the Marangu Route. My wife, April, and I got to know Erick in 2009, and we became friends.

Erick is kind of quiet. He is thoughtful, confident, and he smiles a lot. He is very enjoyable to be around. As we got to know him, we talked about all the people coming to Kilimanjaro and the guidebooks that were then available. We were disappointed that none of them really taught anything about Tanzanian life and culture. They provided little of what someone would need to know to have a great experience when they come to climb Kilimanjaro.

That's how the idea for this book was born. I got a visa for Erick to come to America in 2009, which was not an easy task. He came in 2010 and stayed with us in our home, high up in the mountains of Western Washington, in a small community called Greenwater.

Virtually everything we take for granted in the U.S. or any European country, was a pretty big surprise to Erick. Food everywhere. The washing machines and dryer in our home. Freeways and overpasses. Erick asked me to stop on Interstate 5; he just wanted to get out and take a picture of an overpass. There was nothing that could have possibly prepared him for such a sight in person.

We took him to the Space Needle one night for dinner. That's when I found out that, even though he made his living by guiding people on Kilimanjaro, he was very afraid of heights. We could not get him anywhere near the edge to look down.

We live in a rural mountain community and there are a lot of elk in the area. As you might know, an elk is like a deer, but about five times bigger. Erick knew I had a handgun, since I'm a retired police officer. Upon seeing an elk in my neighborhood, he got very animated and said, "Shoot it! You can shoot it!"

You see, in Tanzania, if an animal wanders into your village, you can kill it and feed many people. God has provided it for you and your neighbors. I explained that we couldn't shoot it, and that we didn't need to do so to have enough food, but I think this was hard for him to understand—to let an opportunity like this to feed the village slip past.

We met up with Phil and Susan Ershler for dinner one night at an upscale restaurant on Elliott Bay in Seattle. Erick knew Phil from climbs and safari trips in Tanzania, where Phil takes clients from his business, International Mountain Guides. Phil is one of the top climbing guides in the world, and he and Susan have climbed the highest peaks on all seven continents as a team. They wrote a book called *Together on Top of the World*. It's a great read.

During dinner, I noticed that Erick kept looking at a nearby table occupied by a Black American couple. I realized that people from Tanzania don't come in contact with many Black Americans. Virtually everything was new to Erick on this trip.

Like I said, you could write an entire book from the perspective of Erick and his trip to America. Before we sent him back to

Tanzania, via San Francisco, London, and Nairobi, we made one last stop on the way. We took him to Disneyland.

It's almost impossible to imagine what this experience was like for Erick. As a child, he lived in a mud and thatched roof beehive hut, with cows and goats brought inside at night to keep everybody warm. He does not live that way today, but at the time he came to America, his house in Moshi didn't even have windows. Imagine going from there to Space Mountain in Disneyland.

Although I strongly suspect Erick was terrified at times, he could never get the smile off of his face. I would ask if he was OK, and he always said he was, but I'm not so sure: sometimes I could hear him say "sheet!" This is kind of a Tanzanian British-accent version of *shit!* At the end of the Hollywood Tower of Terror Hotel ride, I asked him if he had fun. He smiled widely and said "yes." I asked if he wanted to go on it again. He said "no," he was good.

Erick went home and took with him unbelievable memories from America. I think he became something of a celebrity, and people still come to his home to ask to see his photos. He took hundreds of pictures and I printed copies of them for him to take back to Africa.

During our visits, we talked about the existing books on climbing Kilimanjaro. Erick wanted to write a real book for prospective climbers. The more we talked, the better the idea seemed. We agreed to try to get it done someday.

Over time, we finally got the book project done, and there is nothing like it, nor has there ever been. Roughly 50,000 people a year come to Kilimanjaro to attempt the climb. Some should never have come in the first place because they were not ready. The rest had no place to find the proper information they needed to have a successful and culturally fulfilling trip. So much was not being experienced.

Erick's story can change that, along with finally bringing an end to the insulting, inaccurate, and hurtful colonial-era thinking that permeates all prior books on this subject. The earlier writers probably didn't intend to be inaccurate and insensitive. They just didn't know any better and followed the examples of those who had come before them, all the way back to the colonial terrorists who invaded these lands and cultures in East Africa.

We all have a lot to learn from Africa and from the great people of Tanzania. This is their story. This is Erick's story. I really hope you enjoy it. I also hope you have a great trip to Tanzania and to the snows on the very top of Kilimanjaro!

Finally, if this book is successful, Erick might finally get the windows for his house in Moshi. He and his wife also want to visit us in America again. They will be very welcome when they arrive.

ACKNOWLEDGMENTS

Just like climbing Kilimanjaro, no one can do it alone, and so it was with this book. I want to thank my friends, Christopher and April Hurst for their help in getting the story down in writing and ready for editing. April and her friend, Bertha Moore did the excellent maps and charts for the book. The photos are from Christopher Hurst and April Hurst, along with Matt Jones and Lisa Jones from Canada. I really appreciate them. I was also deeply fortunate to have the assistance of Alex Heard from America, who did an outstanding job in editing this book. He is a very creative professional, and I owe much to him. Maria Levin created the cover art from photos that Christopher took on his journeys to East Africa. Frank Yuchymiw of BookBaby has helped us on the journey of self-publishing, something that was new to us. Scott Walker and Tom Irwin took the time to read the entire original manuscript and offered help and support along the way. My family and friends in Tanzania mean so much to me, and I could not have accomplished anything in my life without their support. I am blessed. *Asante Sana* (Thank you very much) to you the reader, for buying and reading my book!